Child Support
and Welfare Reform

Pat Wong

Garland Publishing, Inc.
New York & London
1993

Library of Congress Cataloging-in-Publication Data

Wong, Patrick.
    Child support and welfare reform / Pat Wong.
        p.   cm. — (Children of poverty)
    Revision of thesis (doctoral)—University of Wisconsin.
    Includes bibliographical references (p.   ) and index.
    ISBN 0–8153–1123–0 (alk. paper)
    1. Child support—United States. 2. Child welfare—United States.
I. Title. II. Series.
HV741.W687   1993
362.7'1—dc20   93–16208
                                                            CIP

Printed on acid-free, 250-year-life paper
Manufactured in the United States of America

Contents

Tables

Figures

Preface

More than a fifth of American children live in families with income below the federal poverty line. Children living in single-mother families fare even worse. Their poverty rate is fifty-seven percent. The overwhelming majority of children in single-mother families have a living but absent father. How the country designs the mechanism to ensure the financial support of these children is instrumental to their economic well-being.

The traditional system that implements child support policy is based on the distinction between a judicially based enforcement system of private responsibility, and an entitlement-based financing system of public responsibility. There are many problems with this traditional system, but they boil down to one general theme. The traditional system enforces neither private nor public responsibility effectively.

Welfare reform is in fact this country's repeated attempts to alter how the child support system structures each type of responsibility. In the Great Society era, there was as much political attention on the public as there was on the private side of the responsibility equation. With the subsequent conservative tides, more emphasis was put on enforcing private obligations.

At one level my objective in this book is to examine the substance of this policy. To that end I have described the development of specific provisions in this country's child support system, as well as its most critical issues today. At another level I would like to deal with a normative issue: how the child support system should be structured to enforce the social values that it is supposed to embody. I call this structure the organizational character of the policy.

My hope is to search for a practical way to organize child support policy so that both of the parents of the children involved as well as the public would be encouraged to fulfill social expectations on them. For the noncustodial parent, this means discharging the moral obligation of paying support. For the custodial parent, the expectation is to be self-sufficient. And for the public, the protection of the well-being of the younger generation.

This study grows out of my doctoral study at the University of Wisconsin. I am indebted to Irv Garfinkel, who supervised my research there and taught me most of what I know about this policy area, as well as many things beyond. Chapter three is in particular an expansion of one of the chapters in my dissertation. Many of the ideas (and most of the good ones) in that chapter originated from him. The Appendix, which details the methodology of the micro-simulation evaluation of the Wisconsin Child Support Assurance System, is also adapted from my dissertation. For that methodology, the advice of Irv and Phil Robins was indispensable. The Appendix may be of interest to readers who wish to understand the technical background of the results discussed in chapters 5 and 6.

I started teaching at the LBJ School of Public Affairs shortly before the Family Support Act was passed in 1988. At the LBJ School I have had the opportunity to learn more about issues in policy implementation and administration, for which I am grateful to all my faculty colleagues. I also benefit from the support of the Stephen H. Spurr Centennial Fellowship for the completion of this work. Bee Moorhead, Eliza Gleason, Ping-Wah Li, and Wing-Cheong Lau provided valuable research and editorial assistance. My thanks also go to Betty Godfrey, who spent countless hours typing and reworking the manuscript. Finally, my wife read through several drafts of the manuscript and made numerous constructive comments. Without Stella's editorial assistance and moral support, this book would not have been possible.

Child Support
and Welfare Reform

1

Child Support as a Policy Issue

Child support is at the center of the latest rhetoric on welfare reform. At the 1992 National Convention of the Democratic Party, Governor Bill Clinton had the following message to absent fathers who neglected their child support payments: "Take responsibility for your children or we will force you to do so. Because governments don't raise children; parents do. And you should."[1]

Fulfilling child support obligation--the regular financial payment by a parent to children not living with him or her because of divorce or nonmarital birth--has traditionally been a private issue. Yet society has increasingly felt the need for a concerted policy to *force* noncustodial parents[2] to do so. Perhaps it was the urgency for such a policy that prompted the Governor to give that admonition in the acceptance speech for his presidential nomination, barely one paragraph after he lamented, "Frankly, I'm fed up with politicians in Washington lecturing the rest of us about family values."

The Call for Change

Evidently the moral obligation to pay child support is one family value that is on the mind of many people besides Washington politicians. A few days after the speech the Democratic presidential ticket was in Louisville, Kentucky, as part of the post-convention bus tour. A 16-year-old at a job training center--her name was Deidre Hayes--asked Clinton to crack down on dads who skipped out on their child support.[3] Deidre was speaking about her own father.

On the Republican side and a bit later in the campaign season, President Bush for his part referred constantly to "deadbeat dads" who fail to pay child support. His campaign released a plan that would strengthen child support enforcement.[4] Campaigning as champions of family values, many politicians on the political right found noncustodial parents and child support obligations a natural part of their vocabulary in stump speeches.

Deidre is one of about 16 million children in this country potentially eligible for child support.[5] Most of these children live with their mothers. According to Census survey, in 1990 there were 10 million mothers with children whose fathers were alive but not residing with them. Although society expects these absent fathers to contribute financially to the upbringing of their children, only 44 percent were estimated to have done so in some way.[6] Even among the fathers who did pay child support, just about two-thirds paid the full amount. The other one-third made partial payments only. Among the 56 percent of custodial parents who reported receiving no child support payment, three quarters of them did not even have an officially established child support award.

To be sure, some custodial parents relinquish support awards voluntarily. Other former couples work out joint custody or other private arrangements rendering long-term support payments irrelevant in their mind. Still, in a society where joint custody is uncommon and seldom results in equal sharing of financial obligations,[7] these statistics on delinquent support obligations reflect troubling flaws in our policy. Indeed, of the custodial mothers without child support in 1989, only one-third indicated that they did not want child support payment or did not have one because of other agreement.[8] Public sentiments are ever stronger about the need for change in child support enforcement.

In fact, both major-party presidential candidates were well aware that child support had galvanized political consensus for the last fifteen years. During this period, the system of child support in the United States underwent a series of changes. The intensity of public sentiments and the rapidity of change were both underscored on August 4, 1992, right in the middle of the election campaign, when the U.S. Commission on Interstate Child Support released a lengthy report reviewing the nation's child support system and setting forth recommendations for changes.[9] Within hours of its release, the U.S. House of Representatives passed a bill making interstate flight to avoid child support payments a federal crime.[10]

Children's issues do not usually occupy a prominent place in the American political agenda.[11] Yet when more than half of the children with an absent parent live in poverty,[12] it inevitably catches the attention of the public. The social perception of parental irresponsibility and the extent of child poverty--and their ramifications for the persistence of the underclass--has ignited a lively debate on family values. In this debate, there are two major issues centered around the topic of child support. The first is the morality of single parenthood. This is not the question that will concern us in this book. We will simply observe that divorce and nonmarital births are both facts of modern life. Moral or not, these events have resulted in a population of children living with one parent only.

The second value question is the starting point of the policy inquiry here. It asks how the moral obligations of supporting these children should be exercised by three parties: the noncustodial parent, the custodial parent, and the government.

Child support policy is not just a matter of values either. When the public take a closer look, they do not only see many noncustodial parents failing to live up to society's expectations, they also see an increasing number of children from disrupted families suffering from economic distress. And they see a future for the American society where the younger workforce are not educated and where crimes and other social problems are rampant. In the mind of the public, many of these images can be traced

to indifference about parental responsibility and the
inadequacy of the child support system.

Child support also has implications beyond the
immediate impact of financial payments. Paternity
determination is an essential element in defining support
obligations. It affects children's lineage, self-identity and
hereditary rights later in life. Moreover, eligibility for
health insurance coverage, educational benefits, and
public social services are affected by the design of child
support policy. As will be argued in this book, the structure of the child support system in this country is inexpli-
cably tied to the broader issues of parental obligations and
social expectations on families receiving welfare.

The Dual System of Child Support

This book is an attempt to understand the child
support system: its design in the past, reforms in recent
years, and prospects for its future. The United States has
a dual system of child support. One part of the system is
predicated on the legal dissolution of marriage. In this
part of the system the parties to the disrupted marriage,
either through agreement or court adjudication, set an
amount for child support. This becomes part of the divorce
decree.

Traditionally the enforcement of the agreement is
left to the two parties involved. Because this portion of the
child support system does not involve public financing of
support, we will call it the private child support system.
This system essentially redistributes financial resources
from the noncustodial family to the custodial family.
Until a decade or so ago, government intervention into
private child support was restricted to judicial mechanisms which were largely seen as ineffective.[13] Litigation was the only recourse in this traditional private child
support system.

In contrast, the second part of the child support
system in this country involves public financing. This

public system is triggered, upon application, when a custodial family's economic resources are determined to have fallen below a predetermined government standard established by each state. Custodial families become part of this system when they receive no or insufficient private child support payments, and when the custodial parents' own resources are also inadequate to support the children. This public system of child support takes the form of the Aid to Families with Dependent Children, also known as AFDC or welfare.

The private child support system no longer provides an adequate model today. There are far more family disruptions than the judicial system is equipped to handle. Moreover, many children become eligible for child support not because of divorce, but because of birth outside marriage. There is no established judicial mechanism similar to divorce proceedings that ensures the review of support obligations for them.

Many noncustodial parents do not make their payments voluntarily or are simply financially incapable of providing adequate support. As private support obligations are unfulfilled, the public portion of the system becomes overburdened. This leads to an increasing number of families on welfare, unacceptable level of budget outlays, and public perception of the system as one that discourages the work ethic and perpetuates poverty.

Policymakers realized the anachronism of this dual system more than two decades ago. Changes have occurred in small steps in both the public and private child support systems. Gradually the public support system has shifted from its initial emphasis on helping mothers stay home to a current emphasis on parental obligation to work. In an incremental manner, a bureaucratic mechanism has also been put in place to enforce the private support system.

As a result of these changes, government interventions into the private support system have become increasingly prominent, moving that system from the judicial realm toward the realm of legislative mandates and administrative enforcement. Government mandates on child support have become more universalistic, no longer limited to families relying on public assistance. In this process the private and the public portions of the child support system are more and more intertwined. This historical development will be explored in chapter 2.

This gradual convergence of the dual child support system has led to the policy question of what future steps this nation should take. Chapter 3 sets up a normative framework for evaluating child support policy. It identifies five essential elements required in a comprehensive child support policy. They are: the *establishment of parentage*, to ensure parental rights and obligations for all children; the *determination of support award* that is equitable and adequate; the efficient *collection of payments*; a *public safety-net* for all custodial families to guarantee the children's economic well-beings as well as to encourage self-sufficiency; and a *social support structure* that makes employment and self-sufficiency possible. This framework will help our interpretation of past policy development. It will also aid in structuring our examination of new policy ideas in chapters 4 through 6.

The first three elements in this framework deal with the enforcement aspects of private child support. While recent reforms have addressed many issues within these three elements, some critical issues remain unresolved. Chapter 4 examines these issues and recommends a new organizational structure in the system of child support enforcement.

The public child support system is just as important for children living with one parent only. Experiences in European countries as well as policy proposals entertained by Wisconsin and New York point to the concept of advance maintenance or child support assurance as a possible next step. Child support assurance has the potential of integrating the two parts of the current system, removing both the problem of irregular payments in private support and the disincentives to work in public support. This idea will be discussed in detail in chapter 5.

Another important strategy in child support policy is to increase the reward of work for single parents. Many custodial parents receiving AFDC do not have high enough earnings capacity to make working worthwhile. Subsidizing the earnings or wage rate of custodial parents is a potential way out of this dilemma. At the same time, many critics point out that wage intervention is bound to fail if no support network is in place to enable custodial parents to work. Chapter 6 will examine the government's potential role in providing wage incentives and the support infrastructure for the employment opportunities of custodial parents.

Throughout the examination of the history of reform, the essential elements in designing child support policy, and the latest ideas for change, this book aims to address an overall question: is the current dual system of intervention, based on the enforc ement of private support on the one hand, and the financing of public support on the other, the most effective way of implementing the obligations of noncustodial parents, custodial parents, and the public, towards children? The concluding chapter will comment on this issue.

In order to understand better the debate on child support policy, the remainder of this chapter will be devoted to two background issues. The first issue is the socioeconomic profile of the children who are eligible for child support. The second issue is the nature and problems of this dual system.

Children Eligible for Child Support

A child becomes eligible for child support either through the dissolution of marriage of its parents or through birth out of wedlock. Currently more than a quarter of all children are in this category, compared to only one in ten in 1970. (See Table 1.1.) In fact, this cross-sectional view does not actually represent the extent of the number of children who have ever experienced parental divorce or were born out-of-wedlock. A life-course perspective can better capture this picture. And it is a startling picture indeed: about six out of ten babies born

Table 1.1

Living Arrangement of Children and Parental Marital
Status, 1970, 1980, and 1991

	1970	1980	1991
Total Number	69.16	63.43	69.09

Living Arrangements

Both parents	58.94 (85%)	48.62 (77%)	46.66 (72%)
Mother only	7.45 (11%)	11.41 (18%)	14.61 (22%)
Father only	0.75 (1%)	1.06 (2%)	2.02 (3%)
Other	2.02 (3%)	2.34 (4%)	1.81 (3%)

Parental Marital Status

Among Children Living with Mother Only

Total Number	7.45	11.41	14.61
Never married	0.53 (7%)	1.75 (15%)	5.04 (34%)
Divorced	2.30 (31%)	4.77 (42%)	5.21 (36%)
Separated	3.23 (43%)	3.61 (32%)	3.58 (25%)
Widowed	1.40 (19%)	1.29 (11%)	0.78 (5%)

Among Children Living with Father Only

Total Number	0.75	1.06	2.02
Never married	0.03 (4%)	0.08 (7%)	0.53 (26%)
Divorced	0.18 (24%)	0.52 (49%)	0.92 (46%)
Separated	0.29 (39%)	0.29 (27%)	0.46 (23%)
Widowed	0.25 (33%)	0.18 (17%)	0.11 (5%)

Note: Numbers are reported in million.
Source: U.S. Bureau of the Census, Current Population
Reports, *Marital Status and Living Arrangements, March
1981 (No.372) and March 1991 (No.461)*.

today can expect to live with only one parent some time before becoming adults.[14]

Half a century ago single parenthood was caused mainly by the death of one of the parents. Today marital disruptions and out-of-wedlock births account for the overwhelming majority of the incidence of single parenthood. As shown in Table 1.1, in 1991 only 5 percent of the children under 18 living in single-parent families have a widowed parent. Thus 95 percent of all children living in single-parent families, or almost 16 million, are theoretically eligible for child support.

Within this pool, the proportion from nonmarital births has become increasingly larger, rising from 7 percent with never-married mothers in 1971 to 34 percent in 1991. Excluding widowed families from these percentages, the proportions are 8.7 percent and 36 percent respectively at the two points in time, a four-fold increase in twenty years. Among children with custodial fathers, the proportion whose fathers are never married has a comparable increase during the last two decades.

Since 1970, the number of children living with a never-married mother has increased almost ten times, and those with a divorced mother more than doubled. Interestingly, the number of children living with a never-married or divorced father has gone up seventeen-fold and five-fold respectively. This reflects the recent surge of the number of fathers awarded custody for their children. Even so currently only 12% of children in single-parent families live with their father.

These demographic trends in themselves would not be as significant for social policy had it not been for the economic hardship that had come to be known as "feminization of poverty." The policy concern for children in the child support system is primarily caused by the economic status of single-mother families. Children with a living but absent father are three times as likely as other children to be in poverty.

Economic well-being

The median income of father-only families was $24,171 in 1991, and for mother-only families, $13,012. These figures were 57 and 31 percent, respectively, of the median income of married-couple families with children.[15] However, these percentages convey a distorted picture of the relative consumption capacity of each family type, because single-father families tend to be much smaller in size.

Expressed as income per family member, the average father-headed family has per-capita purchasing power at 85 percent of that of married-couple families, but mother-headed families have per-capita income that is merely 47 percent of that of families headed by two parents. Thus families headed by a single father are much closer in their economic capacity to those headed by a married couple than to those headed by a single mother.

The poverty rate is also much higher among children in mother-only families. Fifty-seven percent of them were poor in 1991, compared to 22 percent of those living with their father only. These rates translate into disproportionately higher child poverty ratio[16] for mother-only families. While children in mother-only families account for just a quarter of all children, they constitute almost half of all children living in poverty.

The potential significance of child support payments to the economic status of these children is underscored by the fact that change in family composition is the major reason mother-headed families are in poverty. Only 12 percent of mother-headed families become poor through the loss of income, while 75 percent fall below the poverty line because of divorce or the birth of an out-of-wedlock child.[17] These are precisely the circumstances under which a family enters the child support system. Sadly, entering that system has become synonymous with being at high risk of becoming poor.

Or, at least, synonymous with being at high risk of a fall in living standard. Between divorced families and families with nonmarital births, the latter are poorer and remain poor longer because never-married custodial mothers tend to be younger and have lower education and job skill levels. Divorced families, on the other hand, typically experience a more dramatic drop in living standard. Nationally, the resource to need ratio of a post-divorce custodial family is only 67 percent of that of the same family before the divorce.[18] Even for middle-class custodial families, this means significant sacrifice in the children's quality of life.

Whether a child enters the child support system because of the divorce of their parents or nonmarital birth, financial payments from the noncustodial parent may mean the difference between adequate and poverty-stricken living standard. Unfortunately the dual system of child support system has not been successful in protecting the economic well-being of these children.

Problems in the Traditional Dual System

Private child support in the traditional dual system is not a dependable source of income. As pointed out at the beginning of this chapter, 42 percent of eligible custodial mothers did not even have a court-ordered child support award in 1989. Among those who had an award, 24 percent never received any payments and another 26 percent received only partial payments.

For those receiving private child support, the national average of receipt was $2,995 in 1989.[19] This means $250 per month for a family of two children and a care-taking parent, hardly adequate income in itself. Worse still, as an aggregate average over the whole year, this figure conceals the fact that child support payments are often erratic, resulting in the lack of economic security for a large number of children.

Flaws in the private system

Thus, the traditional private child support system has several major problems. First, many custodial families simply do not have an award. Since a family must go through the judicial system to obtain an award--and since divorce must be filed through the court--the problem of no award falls predominantly on out-of-wedlock children. In 1990 only 24 percent of child support eligible never-married mothers had an award, compared with 77 percent of divorced mothers.[20] Under the traditional system, there is no mandatory procedural safeguard to adjudicate the economic right of children born out of wedlock.

Second, even if a custodial family has a child support award, the amount is often inadequate. This stems from the fact that the size of the award is left to judicial discretion. Because of crowded dockets, award determination in practice amounts to judicial rubberstamping of private settlements worked out between the parties. Often, issues of house ownership, child custody and visitation rights become bargaining chips in the negotiation. As a result, the amount of long-term payments for children is likely to be under-determined. Indeed, given the certainty of obtaining present control over properties versus future child support payments under the traditional system, it is perhaps prudent in some cases for attorneys to advise their clients to trade child support amount for property settlements.

Another problem, also arising from the discretionary nature of the private child support system, is that inequity often results. Two noncustodial parents in similar economic circumstances may find themselves having very different support obligations, depending on the disposition of the presiding judge or magistrate and the quality of the legal advise they receive.[21]

Finally, the judicial branch has little capacity to enforce child support collection. Traditionally, once an award has been ordered, the case is out of the court system in most states. Private child support payment is handled between the two parents involved. Only when delinquency in payment occurs can a custodial parent go back to court to start a litigation process.[22] This is time-consuming, expensive, and typically of little remedy to the immediate problem of putting food on the table.

Consequently many custodial families write off private child support as unreliable. A large number of custodial parents work. For others who have insufficient skills, or who have no child care, or whose children are too young, the only recourse is the public child support system of AFDC.

Four million family units participated in AFDC in 1990. At least 85 percent of these families were on the program because of the absence of one parent.[23] This group of 3.4 million custodial families represent more than three out of every ten families that are eligible for private child support. Unfortunately this program is ill-equipped as a public child support system.

Origin of the public system

Originally established in 1935, AFDC was not even designed as a public child support system the way it has become today. Divorces and nonmarital births were not major items on the agenda of the Economic Security Commission which drafted the Social Security Act. The Commission thought they were creating under Title IV, Aid to Dependent Children, a federal extension of mother's pension programs already existing in many states. It was to be a federally subsidized, state-administered program to assist primarily low-income children with widowed mothers and only secondarily children deserted by one or more parents.[24]

But the nature of Title IV was drastically altered in 1939 with the creation of survivors insurance as part of the more generous social security program for these widows. Over the following two decades survivors insurance moved practically all the widowed families out of Title IV. As a result of this change, Title IV was left with families of marital disruptions and illegitimate births--and the nation's public child support system was born with all the stigma associated with divorces and illegitimacy.

Then society itself also changed. The rate of nonmarital birth rose steadily after World War II. Divorce rate exploded shortly after, during the decade of the 1960s.[25] These trends resulted in a rapid expansion of the number of custodial families relying on AFDC in an era preceding changes in societal attitudes towards divorces and nonmarital births. This reinforced the stigma attached to Title IV, especially in the South where race became an added dimension in the tension around welfare. In 1951, Governor Herman Talmadge of Georgia expressed the then prevailing view when he stated that he was "willing to tolerate an unwed mother who makes one 'mistake' but not when the mistake is repeated two, three, four or five times."[26]

The historical relationship between the development of Title IV and those demographic trends is very important for the current status of the public child support system. Today divorce and non-marital births per se are no longer frowned upon the way they were in the 1930s. Yet if a parent is divorced or has a non-marital birth *and* also has low-income, then one is stigmatized, not because of divorce or non-marital birth or poverty, but because of the dependence on a stigmatized public support system.

Flaws in the public system

Stigma is one reason why the level of support provided by AFDC is so low.[27] The adequacy of welfare is often criticized by the political left. Benefit levels, set by individual states, are not sufficient to lift needy families in most states out of poverty. The AFDC guarantee for a single-parent family with two children was $372 per month, or 41 percent of the federal poverty line, in the median state in January, 1992.[28] Combined with food stamps, the total amount of public assistance would rise to $647, still less than three-quarters of the poverty level.

Again, the figures for the hypothetical median state masked tremendous variations--some would say inequity-- across states. At the beginning of 1992, the state with the lowest AFDC benefit level (Mississippi) provided $120 a month for a family of three. The most generous state (Alaska), on the other hand, paid $924 to the same family. While AFDC is perceived by the public as expensive and wasteful, the 1990 federal expenditure on AFDC was $11.5 billion, just about 3 percent of total federal outlays for that year.[29]

At the same time, the work disincentives of the program make AFDC even more unpopular politically. As structured, AFDC encourages dependency.[30] Since benefits are reduced as earnings increase, the effect is equivalent to imposing a high tax rate on the earnings of custodial parents. Furthermore, AFDC offers nothing to supplement the incomes of recipients with a low earnings capacity. It is therefore no surprise that fewer than 7 percent of the AFDC heads of families had a full-time or part-time job in 1990, compared to more than twice as many in 1969.[31]

It is also estimated that at any point in time, about half of the caseload of welfare tend to be long-term recipients in the midst of an eight-year or longer episode of continuous receipt of AFDC.[32] This persistent dependency and the increasing outlay of the program have led to the public outcry to reform the system. As Charles Murray put it, "We tried to provide more for the poor and produced more poor instead. We tried to remove the barriers to escape from poverty, and inadvertently built a trap."[33]

This public outcry did not appear as a sudden outburst of public opinions. Rather, dissatisfaction with this dual child support system has been present over the last three decades. Policymakers have attempted to amend the system many times over. Sometimes these reform efforts took place with overall consensus. Other times the policy environment was filled with tension amidst ideological conflicts and competing visions of the ideal system. These battles were all fought under the banner of welfare reform.

The welfare system criticized by Murray and others includes many income-tested programs in addition to AFDC. But in the politics of welfare reform AFDC is always the center of the debate. With AFDC co-opted as a public child support system, however, welfare reform over the past three decades has essentially been about the best way to design the nation's system of child support.[34]

Notes for Chapter 1

1. "Transcript of Speech by Clinton Accepting Democratic Nomination," *New York Times*, July 17, 1992, A14.

2. The terms "noncustodial parents," "absent parents," and "nonresident parents" are used interchangeably in the literature. In this book "noncustodial parents" will be used except when the emphasis is on parental *absence*.

3. "Clinton-Gore Bus Tour Heads for Last Stop," *Austin American-Statesman*, July 22, 1992, A9.

4. "Bush Unveiled Welfare Reform Plan," *Austin American Statesman*, October 12, 1992, A1.

5. U.S. Bureau of the Census, Current Population Reports, Series P-20, No. 461, *Marital Status and Living Arrangements: March 1991* (U.S. Government Printing Office, Washington, D.C., 1992). According to Table 5, p. 39, the total number of children below 18 who were living with only one parent in March 1991 was 16.6 million. Among them 0.8 million were living with widowed parents. Therefore 15.8 million of them were potentially eligible for child support.

6. U.S. Bureau of the Census, Current Population Reports, Series P-60, No. 173, *Child Support and Alimony:*

1989 (U.S. Government Printing Office, Washington, D.C., 1990).

7. While joint legal custody--both parents sharing decision-making authority over children's well-being--has been on the rise, joint physical custody remains relatively rare. Yet it is physical custody that determines which parent bears financial burden. In fact, the 7 percent of custodial mothers reporting joint legal custody arrangement actually had above-average child support receipts. U.S. Bureau of the Census, *Child Support and Alimony, 1989*. See also Judith A. Seltzer, "Legal and Physical Custody Arrangements in Recent Divorces," *Social Science Quarterly* 71 (1990): 250-266.

8. *Ibid.*, p.12, Table I.

9. U.S. Commission on Interstate Child Support, *Supporting Our Children: A Blueprint for Reform* (Washington: Government Printing Office, 1992).

10. H. R. 1241 sponsored by Representative Henry Hyde (R-IL). Its companion bill in the Senate, known as the Shelby bill after the Senator from Alabama, was not taken up by the full Senate in the 102nd Congress.

11. Gilbert Y. Steiner, *The Futility of Family Policy* (Washington: The Brookings Institution, 1981).

12. Mary Jo Bane and David T. Ellwood, "One Fifth of the Nation's Children: Why Are They Poor?" *Science* 245 (1989): 1047-1053.

13. David L. Chambers, *Making Fathers Pay: The Enforcement of Child Support* (Chicago: University of Chicago Press, 1979).

14. Arthur J. Norton and Paul C. Glick, "One-Parent Families: A Social and Economic Profile." *Family Relations* 35 (1986): 9-17. For a range of estimates see also Larry Bumpass, "Children and Marital Disruption: A Replication and Update," *Demography* 21 (1984): 71-81; and Sandra L. Hofferth, "Updating Children's Life Course," *Journal of Marriage and the Family* 47 (1985): 93-115.

15. U.S. Bureau of Census, Current Population Reports, Series P-60, No.180, *Money Income of Households, Families*

and Persons in the United States: 1991 (Washington, DC: Government Printing Office, 1992), pp. 68-69, Table 18.

16. The poverty rate is the percentage of individuals in a specified group who are poor. The poverty ratio is the proportion of poor individuals who belong to the specified group.

17. Mary Jo Bane and David T. Ellwood, "Slipping into and out of Poverty: The Dynamics of Spell," *Journal of Human Resource* 21 (1986): 2-23.

18. Greg J. Duncan and Richard D. Coe, "The Dynamics of Welfare Use," in G. J. Duncan, *Years of Poverty, Years of Plenty* (Ann Arbor MI: Institute for Social Research, 1984).

19. U.S. Bureau of Census, Current Population Reports, *Child Support and Alimony: 1989*, p.1.

20. *Ibid.*, p.5, Table C.

21. Lucy M. Yee, "What Really Happens in Child Support Cases: An Empirical Study of the Establishment and Enforcement of Child Support Awards in the Denver District Court," *Denver Law Journal* 57 (1979): 21-70.

22. David L. Chambers, *Making Fathers Pay: The Enforcement of Child Support* (Chicago, IL: University of Chicago Press, 1979).

23. U.S. House of Representatives, Committee on Ways and Means, *Overview of Entitlement Programs: 1992 Green Book* (Washington DC: Government Printing Office, (1992), p.675.

24. Christopher Howard, "Sowing the Seeds of 'Welfare'" The Transformation of Mothers' Pensions, 1900-1940," *Journal of Policy History*, Vol. 4, No. 2 (1992): 188-227.

25. National Center for Health Statistics, *Vital Statistics of the United States, Vol I, Natality* (Washington DC, various years).

26. Quoted in Winifred Bell, *Aid to Dependent Children* (New York: Columbia University Press, 1965), p. 67.

27. Michael B. Katz, *The Undeserving Poor: From the War on Poverty to the War on Welfare* (New York: Pantheon Books, 1989).

28. The other 15 percent of the families were on AFDC for the following reasons: unemployed parents (5%), incapacitated parent (3%), deceased parent (1.5%), unknown reasons (6%). See U.S. House of Representatives, Committee on Ways and Means, *Overview of Entitlement Programs, 1992 Green Book* (Washington, DC: Government Printing Office, 1992), p.637.

29. *Ibid.*, p.654.

30. June A. O'Neill, Laurie J. Bassi, and Douglas A. Wolf, "The Duration of Welfare Spells" *The Review of Economics and Statistics* (1987): 241-248; Robert Moffitt, "Incentive Effects of the U.S. Welfare System: A Review" *Journal of Economic Literature* 30 (1992): 1-61.

31. *Ibid.*, p.676.

32. Mary Jo Bane and David T. Ellwood, "The Dynamics of Dependence: The Routes to Self-Sufficiency," Prepared for the U.S. Department of Health and Human Services, 1983. In an update to this study, Ellwood found that if multiple episodes of receipt are taken into account, the percentage of long-term recipients would be even higher. See David T. Ellwood, "Targeting the Would-be Long Term Recipient: Who Should Be Served?" Report to the U.S. Department of Health and Human Services (1986).

33. Charles Murray, *Losing Ground: American Social Policy, 1950-1980* (New York: Basic Books, 1984).

34. One exception has been the extension of AFDC benefits to unemployed two-parent families with children in 1988. Since over half the states already had AFDC-U prior to that date and since eligibility is time-limited, that change is not expected to have a significant impact on the welfare system. Major changes in "welfare" have in fact occurred in expansion of medicaid eligibility. That development is generally thought of as health care reform rather than welfare reform.

2

Recent Reforms of the Child Support System

The history of reform in the nation's dual child support system is a history of the triumph of "muddling through" over the "rational-comprehensive approach" to policy decision-making.[1] In a classic critique of the latter approach, Charles Lindblom argued that political, institutional and cognitive limitations prevent us from adopting optimization as a decision strategy. Rational optimization requires unambiguous consensus on value priorities as well as comprehensive comparison of all potential policy options, neither of which is tenable in reality.

Instead, the only practical strategy to policy development is to ignore all but one or two social objectives and to restrict attention to a few feasible options. Consequently, reform efforts that work tend to be incremental changes in a limited number of program features. These changes are often the result of the prevailing political wind of the time rather than that of scientific knowledge and planning.

Since the establishment of the AFDC system in 1935, U.S. child support policy has undergone numerous waves of reform. "Welfare reform" has been the battle cry used by every policymaker attempting to change the nation's system of financial support for children in single-headed families. This battle cry took on different meanings in different eras, however. For example, until the middle of the 1970s, reformers' energy was directed primarily at the public child support system of AFDC. Since that time, "welfare reform" more often than not referred to the tinkering with the private child support system.

Tinkering is the appropriate word to describe the development of policies on private child support. For these changes have followed a logic of incremental muddling ever since the first enactment of the federal law on private support enforcement in 1950. For the past forty years, changes were made--first very slowly, then acceler-ated after the mid-1970s--to alter the mechanism of decision-making and enforcement in the private child support system.

Incremental tinkering can add up if they are driven by consistent value objectives and based on the institution-al learning that accompanies the changes. Together and over time, the experiences of tinkering have resulted in significant changes in the private child support system, moving it from a system of judicial discretion and volun-tary compliance toward a system of uniform admin-istration and mandatory compliance. Before delving into the metamorphosis of the private support system, however, it is important also to look at the reform efforts on public child support. For changes in public child support consti-tute a story of contrast in the theory of muddling through.

Reform Efforts in Public Child Support

Over the past half century, there were many serious attempts at overhauling the public child support system, especially from the late 1960s to the middle of 1970s. These included a series of negative income tax experi-ments in an effort to ascertain the optimal level of benefits and program structure, and actual proposals such as the Family Assistance Plan suggested by the Nixon Administration and the Program for Better Job and Income introduced by the Carter Administration.[2] These efforts were bold moves that attempt to optimize the value objectives of providing adequate income, minimizing work disincentives, and containing program costs all at the same time.

As comprehensive changes in welfare policy, these programs had one thing in common. They all failed. For example, the Family Assistance Plan proposed a nationally uniform minimum income guarantee to families with dependent children, at $1,600 per annum for a family of four in 1969. The bill was repeatedly rejected by the Senate. Finally, the provisions dealing with the elderly and the disabled in the original plan were approved as the supplemental security income (SSI) program in 1972. The proposed uniform benefit for children was dropped.[3] A key difference between SSI and welfare reform was the long-held consensus that the elderly and the disabled were deserving poor. Without passing the "deserving poor" test, programs for custodial families do not have the requisite political support for comprehensive reform.

Incremental changes

Instead, successful changes in the public child support program have typically been incremental changes in benefit levels, work requirements, and administrative procedures. As Garfinkel points out, when the prevailing sentiments from 1955 to 1975 were to increase economic security for single-mother families, AFDC benefit levels kept rising. As the national mood reversed itself after 1975 and as welfare reduction became the dominant objective, benefits were cut and eligibility became more restrictive.[4]

Another incremental strategy was also important in expanding access to AFDC. During the 1950s and 1960s, welfare activists successfully used outreach campaigns and litigations to reduce governmental discretion in disqualifying recipients. These reform efforts made the public child support system more accessible to custodial families and played a role in the expansion of welfare in the 1960s.[5] These efforts reached their limits when eligibility determination became relatively standardized and when the public's concern shifted from inadequate program access to problems of fraud and irresponsibility.

Work expectations

The increasing caseload of able-bodied but non-working AFDC custodial parents had become a concern in the beginning of the Kennedy years. Attention began to focus on how the structure of the program might have discouraged work. At the beginning AFDC benefits were reduced dollar for dollar by earnings, with no allowance for expenses related to work. The Social Security Amendment of 1962 introduced the deductibility of work-related expenses, and ushered in the era of "work incentives" to welfare reform.[6] Accompanying this change was an emphasis on social and counseling services to help make welfare recipients job-ready, a process called "reformation by rehabilitation" by some observers.[7] State welfare programs were permitted to enroll welfare participants in these programs at state discretion.

Additional incentives for work were built into the structure of AFDC in 1967, when the work incentive program (WIN) was authorized. It made further funds available to states for job search and training of welfare recipients. Established during the high tide of the welfare rights movement, WIN was perceived by critics on the left as another device to keep single parents from obtaining public assistance. The WIN program was consequently decried as "WIP" instead. But it was clear by then that the work incentive strategy to welfare reform was here to stay.

Also introduced in the amendment was the "thirty-and-a-third" rule whereby welfare recipients were allowed to have the first thirty dollars and one third of the rest of the monthly earnings net of work expenses excluded from family resources in calculating the amount of benefits. This procedure reduced the effective tax rate of work while receiving public child support dramatically. This new tax rate was still high relative to that faced by persons not on welfare, but it was a significant reduction from the previous rate. The drawback, of course, was that the rule effectively increased the income limit for eligibility, making more families eligible for welfare. Welfare became more costly to the public.

WIN was conceived as a voluntary program to facilitate the custodial parent's transition from dependency to work. As political view began to emphasize parental responsibility in subsequent years, however, WIN turned into a requirement to register for work. This occurred in 1972 with the Talmadge Amendment.

The requirement sent an unmistakable message to welfare recipients about the shift in public expectations. The substantive impact of the Talmadge Amendment, however, was minimal. The inadequate funding of WIN, the unavailability of jobs suitable for AFDC parents, and the large number of custodial parents exempted because of the presence of a child under six years of age made the number of families moving off AFDC as a result of these policy changes very small.

In fact, when the Reagan Administration took office in 1981, time limit was imposed on the thirty-and-one-third deduction rule and its computation was made less generous.[8] Such incentives were seen as ineffective.[9] Instead, the Administration proposed direct work requirements so that welfare recipients must work in exchange for benefits. This proposal finally became state options in the 1981 Omnibus Budget Reconciliation Act.

With the Reagan philosophy of making custodial parents work for AFDC, the transformation of the public child support system from one based on "maternal ethic" to one based on "work ethic" was complete. While the philosophical emphasis on work ethic was clear, the actual organizational commitments to that emphasis was far less so. Adequate resources were never provided to assist the custodial families in gaining financial independence. Therefore the transformation of philosophy in the public support system remains an abstract idea, at least until the

Family Support Act of 1988, when some support structure began to accompany the work requirements.

This transformation from maternal to work ethic was rooted in the solidifying of public expectation on parental responsibility. The changes in the public child support system, however, covered only half of the expectation--the half upon the custodial parents. Society clearly also expects the noncustodial parents to fulfill their parental obligations. That expectation was embodied in the reform in private child support.

Early Reforms in Private Child Support

As political attention turned to the role of the noncustodial parents, the private child support system became the centerpiece of welfare reform with the passage of a major amendment to the Social Security Act in 1975. Just as the strategy of requiring custodial parents to work for public child support took two decades to build up, the strategy of child support enforcement did not come into being overnight. Three inconspicuous pieces of federal legislation targeting private child support had been enacted in the preceding twenty-five years.

As it became clear in 1950 that AFDC was emerging as the public child support system for children with living but absent parents, the federal government made its first attempt to hold noncustodial parents accountable for the financial well-being of their children. That year Congress passed the Notice to Law Enforcement Officials Amendment to Title IV of the Social Security Act. The amendment required state welfare agencies to notify law enforcement officials when a family with a child deserted by a parent was enrolled in AFDC. It was, however, up to local prosecutors whether to pursue deserting parents. Since there was no requirement nor incentive for prosecutors to follow up on the reports, however, this amendment had virtually no effect in practice.

Congress revisited private child support in 1965. By then political leaders had recognized the importance of placing in the hands of the state welfare bureaucracy-- which had a stake in containing welfare expenditures-- rather than the law enforcement bureaucracy, the responsibility of pursuing noncustodial parents. With the passage of P.L. 89-97, states and local welfare agencies were authorized to obtain from the then U.S. Department of Health, Education, and Welfare, the address and employment information of any noncustodial parent whose children received AFDC and who owed child support under a court order.

The weakest link in child support enforcement did not lie with noncustodial parents with a court-ordered obligation, however. It was the fathers of children born out of wedlock that were the most difficult to locate and their legal responsibility the hardest to establish. Moreover, it was realized that the mere acquisition of information on noncustodial parents did not by itself lead to payments by these parents. The enormous number of noncustodial parents and the existing workload of the local welfare agencies called for a designated organizational unit with the mandate to pursue these parents.

Thus materialized the third passed at incremental change, when Congress passed P.L. 90-248. This amendment in 1967 required states to designate an agency for paternity establishment and support collection. These state agencies were to cooperate with one another in interstate enforcement of child support payment. Paternity determination had by now become a mandate rather than an option for children receiving AFDC benefits.

These three pieces of early legislation culminated in a rudimentary system of state-level organizational units with a limited mission. The agencies were organized specifically around the public child support system. Their mission was restricted to identifying the noncustodial parents of children relying on public support. Upon identification, these parents were channeled back to the traditional judicial system for paternity and support determination. And this state-level enforcement system

was not particularly effective. As Gilbert Steiner describes
it, the early "federal policy amounted to little more than
a polite request to states that they request deserting
fathers to make child support payments."[10]

These early attempts by the federal government
reflected the institutional principles prevalent at the time.
First, the private child support system was to remain the
prerogatives of the states. Even though Congress saw fit
to pursue noncustodial parents when public monies were
used to support their children, the federal government
refrained from taking a leadership role in enforcing child
support. Consequently the limited mandates in these three
pieces of legislation were not matched with any coordination and hardly any financial resources from the federal
government.

The second principle reflected in the early reforms
was equally significant: a distinction was to be drawn
between the noncustodial parents whose children relied on
public child support and those who did not. Limited as the
federal mandates were regarding the former, there was to
be no federal intervention at all regarding the private
support practices of the latter.

These two principles would later be partially super-
ceded by later legislation. Yet the distinction between
AFDC and non-AFDC cases has nonetheless persisted even
today as the conceptual framework in organizing the child
support enforcement system. While the scope of these early
reform measures was limited, they constituted an important part of the process of muddling through. This process
resulted in institutional learning that made further
evolution of child support policy possible.

Bureaucratization of Support Enforcement

By the second Nixon Administration, the attempt to
overhaul the public child support system--the Family
Assistance Plan--had proved to be futile. With the failure
of comprehensive reform, the concern of the general

public shifted from the provision of adequate economic protection for children to the containment of the public support system from further expansion. Reducing the level of benefits was one strategy, but dramatic reduction of benefits was politically unpopular. In any case that strategy was not available to the federal government since benefits were set by the states. The alternative was to lessen the burden on the public treasury by collecting more payments from the noncustodial parents.

Thus the political context was ripe for targeting the responsibility of the noncustodial parents in welfare reform. By this time the experience from the previous legislative efforts to track down noncustodial parents had also made some lessons clear. To pursue private child support obligations effectively, the federal government must provide not only information, but also the organizational leadership and financial resources. As a result, the Child Support Enforcement Amendment, known as Title IV-D of the Social Security Act, was signed into law in 1975.

Institutionalizing bureaucratic enforcement

The creation of Title IV-D commenced the adoption of private child support enforcement as a welfare reform paradigm. A federal Office of Child Support Enforcement (OCSE) was established within the Department of Health, Education, and Welfare. OCSE was charged with the responsibility to coordinate, monitor, and evaluate state programs as well as to provide technical assistance.

The state network of agencies previously designated to pursue AFDC noncustodial parents were charged with locating noncustodial parents, bringing them to court for paternity adjudication, obtaining court-ordered child support awards, collecting and disbursing payments, and assisting in suits against parents who were delinquent in payment on behalf of the custodial families. The federal government would, under Title IV-D, provide these state programs with a 75 percent matching fund. In a significant broadening of mission, the state programs now had the mandate to work not only with AFDC custodial families, but also, upon request, with non-AFDC custodial families.

In addition, P.L. 93-647 also provided for federal incentive payments to states in accordance with their performance in collecting private payments on behalf of AFDC custodial families. The rationale was that incentive payments would encourage collections, which would in turn reduce AFDC caseload and expenditures.

The 1975 Amendment was the prototype of fiscal federalism. It established the nation's federal-state administrative organizational network in private child support policy that still exists today. Most states have set up their state enforcement agency within the department administering the public child support program, but a few states operate their IV-D programs out of the Department of Revenue or Attorney General's Office.

The institutionalization of this enforcement network, infused with newly available financial resources made possible by federal matching funds, ushered in a period of experimentation on various techniques of child support enforcement. The successful techniques were then adopted into legislation. One of the first group of such techniques found their way into the Omnibus Budget Reconciliation Act (P.L. 97-35) of 1981. They included authorization for the Internal Revenue Service to withhold federal income tax refunds for delinquent noncustodial parents with children on AFDC, and prohibition of the discharge of child support obligations in bankruptcy proceedings.

With the creation of the enforcement bureaucracy and the development of organizational capacity for collection, aggregate child support payment for AFDC recipients increased 280 percent between 1976 and 1985.[11] The private child support enforcement (IV-D) functions were now formally established within public administration, but it was to be separated from the public child support financing function of the AFDC (IV-A) program.

Legislative reinforcement

Whatever the degree of success in collections, the private system was still plagued by two shortcomings: the failure to obtain support awards in a large portion of potentially eligible cases and the gross inadequacy of the amount of the awards themselves. In 1984, the Child Support Enforcement Amendments (P.L. 98-378) were passed to address these issues. The arrival of a consensus on child support reform was affirmed by the unanimous passage of this legislation by Congress.

On the first issue of obtaining awards for child-support-eligible families, the amendments required the states to adopt "expedited procedures" in the judicial or administrative system. This was an acknowledgement of the lack of capacity in handling child support cases by the traditional judicial system. In addition, to facilitate paternity adjudication in cases involving nonmarital birth, states were required to lengthen the statutes of limitation to allow paternity adjudication until a child's eighteenth birthday.

To ensure an adequate amount of support, states were to establish statewide numeric guidelines for judges and magistrates in award adjudications. To reinforce the gains in collections, moreover, the amendment required states to adopt into their enforcement repertoire another group of implementation techniques. Foremost among them was mandatory wage withholding. This provision would apply to cases under OCSE jurisdiction upon one-month of nonpayment. Other implementation techniques required by the 1984 amendment included extension of federal income tax refund interception to non-AFDC noncustodial parents in delinquency, placing liens on property, and reporting delinquent child support debts to credit agencies.

With respect to the fiscal relationship between the federal government and state bureaucracies, the 1984 legislation reduced the federal matching rate for administering Title IV-D to 66 percent by 1990.[12] It also altered the structure of federal incentive payments for state collection performance. Whereas before 1984 incentive payments were based on collections in AFDC cases only, the new federal incentives applied equally to AFDC and non-AFDC collections. This was to signal that enforcement of child support payments for children not receiving public support should be as much the domain of administrative enforcement as those receiving AFDC.

Many of the provisions in the 1984 Amendments were predicated on state laws being in conformity with the federal requirements. For the first time in the development of policy on child support enforcement, states were required not only to strengthen their administrative apparatus, but also to adopt new legislation or modify their existing statutes. This undertaking was quite involving. One can get a flavor of the dynamics of this process by looking at mandatory income withholding as an example.

The General Accounting Office has broken the single provision on mandatory wage withholding down into thirty-nine specific procedures with legislative implications for each state. Among them, thirteen major procedures were reported by GAO:[13]

(1)	Withholding is automatic, not requiring a return to court to change the support order;
(2)	Withholding is triggered when payments are one-month delinquent;
(3)	Withholding applies to interstate as well as intrastate cases;
(4)	The state has a mechanism to document and monitor the withheld amounts;
(5)	Withholding applies to AFDC cases;
(6)	Withholding applies to non-AFDC cases on Title IV-D;
(7)	Withholding applies to foster care cases;
(8)	Withholding applies to interstate cases;
(9)	The amount withheld covers current support as well as payment toward liquidation of arrearage;
(10)	The only bases for contesting are mistakes of fact;
(11)	An advance notice to the absent parent is sent on the trigger date;
(12)	In contested cases, notification on resolution must be sent to the absent parent within 45 days;

(13)   The same notice must also be sent to the employers within 45 days.

The enormous tasks of passing state laws and setting up the corresponding administrative apparatus had caused substantial delay in the initial implementation of the 1984 Amendment.[14] In fact, for some states the process may have been even more complicated than passing new law. Some states like Texas had to pass a constitutional amendment to make automatic wage withholding for child support possible.

That the reform was passed unanimously in spite of the anticipated complications for states was a political victory for advocates of private child support reform. The amendments in 1984 had set the stage for further changes. But before we move forward in this history, three underlying themes within this emerging paradigm--holding noncustodial parents responsible--for welfare reform need to be identified.

Major themes

First, the system of private child support has gradually moved away from judicial discretion toward standardization and centralization. Both the explosion in caseload and the development in collection technology have transformed private support enforcement from a purely judicial system to a primarily judicial system coupled with a loose network of administrative agencies (federal and state OCSE's), and further on to an administrative system backed up by legislative guidelines. At a time when political candidates campaign against government bureaucracy, child support is one system that moves toward bureaucratization.

Second, a symbolic statement on the primacy of parental obligation has been formulated. Before the mid 1970's, debates on welfare issues were centered around how generous the government should be. Gradually, child support enforcement shifted this focus to the extent the noncustodial parents ought to be responsible. While "going after" the noncustodial parents of AFDC families who tend to be of limited means themselves may not be the most cost-effective strategy, the development of the enforcement bureaucracy and legislation has put together an unequivocally affirmative response to the question: "Shouldn't low-income fathers support their children"?[15]

Third, although the use of support enforcement services were mandatory for AFDC custodial families and voluntary for non-AFDC families, the development in child support enforcement up to 1984 had helped increase the average income only for the non-welfare custodial families seeking service. For example, in 1985, OCSE collected $1.7 billion on behalf of non-welfare custodial families. In contrast, collections on behalf of AFDC families, totaling about $1 billion, never reached the custodial families themselves. They were instead used to reimburse IV-A expenditures. Since AFDC recipients did not benefit from increased collection at all, it is not an inaccurate observation that the economic well-being of poor families was not on the agenda of the enforcement strategy.

This was partially changed in 1984 by the Deficit Reduction Act. Congress at that time was concerned about the large number of never-married welfare recipients whose ex-partners were not paying support either because paternity had not been established or because they could not be located. In order to obtain better cooperation from the recipients in locating noncustodial parents and establishing paternity, the first $50 of the child support collected each month is disregarded for the purpose of calculating AFDC grant. The hope was that this new law would provide an incentive for custodial parents to participate in enforcing private child support.[16]

Yet the ultimate anti-poverty effect of such an increase in private child support payment is limited.[17] In fact, the disregard rule is antithetical to the objective of reducing welfare caseload because the disregard rule has in effect lowered the eligibility standard and thus has retained more families in the welfare system.[18]

The Family Support Act of 1988

Political pressure against welfare dependency did not subside with the reform in 1984. Quite the contrary, the establishment of the IV-D bureaucracy and legislative mandates added to demands for more changes. Congress was looking for additional measures that would incorporate both noncustodial parent obligations and custodial parent self-sufficiency. Senator Moynihan of New York, in particular, took the leadership in attempting to replace the existing welfare system with new legislation.[19] In this environment, the Family Support Act was passed in October 1988 as P.L.100-485.

Custodial parents' responsibility to be self-sufficient is addressed in the Job Opportunities and Basic Skills Training Program (JOBS) component of the Act. The new law requires the states to enroll a minimum proportion of custodial parents in various educational, training, and job search programs. Case management and client assessment services are strengthened. While work incentives program in the past could be administered by either the state welfare agency or state employment agency, JOBS must be administered by the welfare agencies.

The Family Support Act also defines the public's role in facilitating employment opportunities for custodial parents. That role includes the provision of child care and medical coverage, even for a transitional period after a custodial parent has become financially independent of the public child support system. Open-ended federal matching funds are made available to states for child care services.

Noncustodial parents' obligations are set forth in provisions governing private child support in the Family Support Act. Not surprisingly, on many issues this legislation picks up where the 1984 Amendment left off. It pushes the private enforcement system further away from

judicial discretion and further towards a model of bureaucratization and standardization.

Paternity establishment

The Family Support Act stipulates both performance
standards and financial penalties as incentives to improve
states' performance in establishing paternity. The law uses
as performance measure the proportion of IV-D nonmarital birth cases in which paternity has been successfully
established. This proportion must be 50 percent, or be at
least the average among all states, or has improved by 3
percentage points each year for a state to be eligible for
the matching grants.

Further, there is a simple requirement that the social
security number of each parent be furnished upon the
birth of an infant. With this requirement, informal
paternity identification becomes a required step in
nonmarital births, and, if it becomes necessary, the future
location of the identified parent is made easier.

Child support standards

Although the 1984 Amendment required the states to
develop numeric guidelines for the amount of award, the
courts were free to set child support awards at levels
different from the guidelines because the guidelines were
merely advisory in nature. The 1988 reform makes the
guidelines rebuttable presumptions. That is, judges may
depart from the formula only for good reasons. In addition, there is now a stipulation of periodic review of the
appropriateness of an award amount at least every three
years. The triennial review is mandatory for families
receiving public child support. It is also required in non-
AFDC cases upon the request of one of the parents.

The rebuttable presumption requirement reinforces
the movement of the private child support system towards

a model of standardization. Most of the child support standards adopted by states can be conceptualized as a child support tax on the noncustodial parents, sometimes with cost-sharing features, taking into account the income of both parents.[20]

Income withholding

While the 1984 Amendment required income withholding *upon a month's delinquency* in payment, the new law provides that, with one important exception, income withholding becomes *universal and automatic* upon the entry of child support award. This provision became effective in November 1990 for new and newly revised cases within the jurisdiction of the IV-D programs. For families that are not under OCSE, the effective date is January of 1994 to allow states the requisite time for implementation.

The one exception to automatic income withholding is when both parents agree to a waiver in court. This alleviates the concern for privacy of some noncustodial parents as long as payment is regular. On the other hand, it can become a loophole when automatic wage withholding, like the amount of child support in the old system, is easily traded away for other items during divorce negotiations.

Automation of procedures

In addition to the improvements in the three areas mentioned, the 1988 welfare reform also contains general requirements on the swiftness of child support enforcement services delivery. Financial incentives in the form of higher federal matching rate, at 90 percent, are offered to the states for the development of automated tracking and monitoring systems by 1995.

Part of the difficulty in administering the traditional private child support system is its fragmentation of
information. With the center of that system in the local
courthouse, there used to be a lack of coordination among
enforcement agencies. The establishment of a management
information system is another step towards a bureaucracy-
based, coordinated model of private child support policy.

Welfare Reform by Revision

Some critics have viewed policy development such as
the Family Support Act as merely welfare revision.[21]
While that assessment is undoubtedly correct when one
piece of amendment is examined in isolation, the history
of welfare reform as a whole shows substantial changes in
how the system is organized.

In the private child support system, the process of
muddling through has resulted in an administrative
apparatus for enforcing parental obligation, at least with
regard to the obligation of noncustodial parents. Reform
in the public child support system began earlier in history
but has lagged behind in accomplishing substantive
organizational changes.

A major difference between the reform experience in
the two components of the child support system is value
consensus. Private child support did not become an
important piece of the reform puzzle until the early 1970s.
When it did, however, there was little dispute about the
efficacy of enforcing noncustodial parent obligations. The
only resistance to the enforcement strategy came, at an
initial implementation of IV-D, from the federal welfare
bureaucracy which did not relish the shift from benefit-
dispensing to monitoring noncustodial parents.[22] Even
there, the resistance dissipated early in the Carter Administration. The public as well as the policy community
arrived at a quick consensus on enforcing noncustodial
parent responsibility.[23] Society was much more ambiva-

lent toward the objective of imposing work expectations on custodial parents.

With the consensus on values, the incremental process in private child support reform succeeded in addressing the substantive organizational apparatus in each round of change. In contrast, the energy in the public child support reform movements were directed at gradually building up social expectations of work obligations on custodial parents. The absence of accompanying organizational resources, however, rendered changes in work requirements ineffective.

The Family Support Act, however, has been heralded as a new consensus on the welfare to work stratey.[24] It has introduced some bureaucratic support for custodial parent self-sufficiency, including child care, medical coverage, as well as case management and better interagency coordination. If this is the beginning of a process of revision in the underlying structure of the public child support system, it is possible that the structural features for self-sufficiency could be developed some time in the future. As evidenced in private child support enforcement, the history of child support reform has been a process of reform through revisions.

This consensus on reforming the public child support system remains weak.[25] As Paul Offner, Senator Moynihan's leislative assistant, observes, "What it boils down to is that everyone is for welfare until they realize how much it costs."[26] Nonetheless, there are signs that the process of revision will continue. Amidst the rhetoric on child support reform in the campaign for his election, President Clinton proposed changing the AFDC system so that families would be offered employment instead of cash assistance after two years of benefits.

New proposals have also been introduced in Congress to establish new mandates on how the child support system should operate. One of the major proposals is the Downey-Hyde Child Support Enforcement and Assurance Proposal, which was unveiled by the two congressmen in the summer of 1992. It would centralize and standardize the enforcement bureaucracy further by federalizing many of the enforcement functions.

The development of the organizational mechanisms for the enforcement of obligations does not necessarily mean that the mechanisms are performing at a satisfactory level, however. In fact, arguments can be made on both sides about whether the bureaucratization movement is a good idea. The next chapter will present some of these arguments.

Notes for Chapter 2

1. Charles E. Lindblom, "The Science of Muddling Through," *Public Administration Review* 19 (1957): 79-88.

2. Leslie Lenkowsky, *Politics, Economics and Welfare Reform: The Failure of the Negative Income Tax in Britain and the United States* (Lanham MD: University Press of America, 1986).

3. Vincent J. Burke and Vee Burke, *Nixon's Good Deed* (New York, NY: Columbia University Press, 1974); Daniel Patrick Moynihan, *The Politics of a Guaranteed Income* (New York, NY: Vintage Books, 1973).

4. Irwin Garfinkel, "Bringing Fathers Back In: The Child Support Assurance Strategy," *The American Prospect* 9 (1992): 74-83. See also Charles Murray, *Losing Ground: American Social Policy, 1950-1980* (New York NY: Basic Books, 1984) for a discussion on the "benefit increase" phase of AFDC; and Tom Joe and Cheryl Rogers, *By the Few, For the Few: The Reagan Welfare Legacy* (Lexington MA: Lexington Books) for an emphasis on the "benefit reduction" phase.

5. Megan H. Morrissey, "The Downtown Welfare Advocate Center: A Case Study of a Welfare Rights Organization," *Social Service Review* 64 (1990): 189-202.

6. Joel F. Handler, *Reforming the Poor: Welfare Policy, Federalism, and Morality* (New York, NY: Basic Books, 1972), p.40.

7. *Ibid.*, p.47.

8. Under the Reagan reform in 1981, the "thirty and one-third" rule applied only in the first four months of AFDC recipiency. Moreover, this disregard rule is based on earnings after child care and work expenses deduction, rather than on gross earnings as before. Child care and work expenses are treated as fixed amounts. Earned income tax credit amount was also figured into the AFDC benefit computation.

9. The ineffectiveness of earnings disregard in increasing work was recognized not only by political conservatives in the Reagan administration, but also by some academic analysts. See Frank Levy, "The Labor Supply of Family Heads, or AFDC Work Incentives Don't Work Too Well," *Journal of Human Resources* 14 (1979): 76-97.

10. Gilbert Y. Steiner, *The Futility of Family Policy* (Washington, DC: Brookings Institution, 1981, p.117.

11. The figure is derived from *Child Support Enforcement Statistics Fiscal Year 1985*, Vol. II, Table 1, and *Child Support Enforcement*, Fifth Annual Report to the Congress for the Period Ending September 30, 1980, Table 2. (Rockville, Md.: National Child Support Enforcement Reference Center).

12. The matching rate was set at 75 percent by the 1975 Amendment. It was changed to 70 percent in 1981. The 1984 Amendment further reduced it to 68 percent in 1988 and 66 percent in 1990.

13. U.S. General Accounting Office, *Child Support: State's Progress in Implementing the 1984 Amendments* (Washington DC: GAO, October 1986).

14. *Ibid.*

15. Blanche Bernstein, "Shouldn't low-income fathers support their children?" *Public Interest* 66 (1982): 55-71.

16. In fact, there was a provision in the 1975 Amendment to disregard, for AFDC purpose, 40% of private child support up to a maximum of $20 per month. It was introduced as an experimental measure for a limited duration. It expires quietly the following year without much public attention.

17. Donald T. Oellerich, *The Effects of Potential Child Support Transfers on Wisconsin AFDC Costs, Caseloads and Recipient Well-being* (Madison WI: University of Wisconsin, Institute for Research on Poverty, Special Report, 1984); Philip K. Robins, "Child Support, Welfare Dependency, and Poverty," *American Economic Review* 76 (1986): 768-788.

18. Irwin Garfinkel, Sara McLanahan, and Pat Wong, "Child Support and Dependency," in Harrel R. Rodgers, ed., *Beyond Welfare: Alternative Approaches to the Problem of Poverty in America* (Armonk, N.Y.:M. E. Sharpe, 1988).

19. U.S. Senate, Committee on Finance, *Welfare Reform: Reform or Replacement?* Hearings before the Subcmmittee on Social Security and Family Policy, 100th Cong., 1st Sess., January 23, February 2, February 20, 1987.

20. For a detailed discussion of the major types of guidelines in use, see Robert G. Williams, *"Guidelines for Setting Levels of Child Support Orders" Family Law Quarterly*, 21 (1987): 281-325; Andrea Giampetro, "Mathematical Approaches to Calculating Child Support Payments: Stated Objectives, Practical Results, and Hidden Policcies" *Family Law Quarterly*, 20 (1986): 373-391.

21. Catherine S. Chilman, "Welfare Reform or Revision? The Family Support Act of 1988," *Social Service Review 66* (1992): 349-377.

22. Gilbert Y. Steiner, *The Futility of family Policy*, pp. 118.

23. See, for example, Michael Novak et al., *The New Consensus on Family and Welfare* (Washington, DC: American Enterprise Institute, 1987).

24. Lawrence Mead, "The Changing Agenda of Welfare Reform in the United States, 1967-88" (Paper presented at the annual conference of the American Political Science Association, San Francisco, August 1990). For the consensus among analysts, see Michael Wiseman,

ed., "Research and Policy: A Symposium on the Family Support Act of 1988" *Journal of Policy Analysis and Management* 10 (1991): 588-666.

25. Mary Bryna Sanger, "The Inherent Contradiction of Welfare Reform" *Policy Studies Journal* 18 (1990): 663-680.

26. Paul Offner, "Workfail: Waiting for Welfare Reform" *The New Republic* 207 (December 28, 1992): 13-15.

3

A Normative Framework for Child Support Policy

> If any proposition would receive an extraordinary
> high affirmative vote in a national poll, it is that parents
> are responsible for the care and support of their children if
> they are physically, mentally, and financially able to be. In
> particular, the father is regarded as having this obligation,
> whether he is present in the house or not.[1]

A nation's child support policy reflects its public philosophy in balancing three often competing values. One value is the long-cherished maxim that parents should provide for their own children. Another social objective, derived as much from the economic as from the humanistic imperative, dictates that society should protect the well-being of its young members when parental support is lacking. Finally, as in any other policy issue faced by the modern capitalist democracy, there is the public value of government efficiency and cost containment.

These three virtues of parental obligation, social responsibility, and budgetary minimalism create fundamental tensions. The dual system has been the United States' response to this tension. Until two decades ago, parental obligation was nominally enforced through judicial mechanisms in the private child support system, while public responsibility was fulfilled first through mother's pension programs and subsequently through AFDC in the public child support system.

So long as the population affected by this dual system remained small, the public's concern about cost and efficiency did not set in. That was why the problems of this dual system went unnoticed for decades. As cost containment became an increasingly serious political constraint, however, public debates emerged with respect to the efficacy of this system.

This chapter considers the first two values of parental responsibility and the government's role in children's well-being in relation to the child support system. If the traditional dual system--judicial discretion combined with public welfare--cannot implement parental and public responsibilities simultaneously and efficiently, is there another approach within which a child support system can be designed to meet these goals?

The section below provides the conceptual arguments that a system of child support should be and can be designed both to enforce parental responsibility and to ensure children's well-being. The rest of the chapter then proceeds to construct such a system by considering the essential policy elements.

Obligations and Policy Design

In a comparative study on child support policy, Alfred Kahn and Sheila Kamerman observe that European nations have had a long tradition of guaranteeing children's well-being.[2] This tradition explains the generous public benefits in European child support systems which, the authors claim, have relatively ignored private support collection. On the other hand, the United States has emphasized parental responsibility by making private support an issue of debt collection. Kahn and Kamerman advocate the move of the U.S. system of child support "from debt collection to social policy" in the interest of the children.

Given the dismal past performance of the private child support enforcement mechanism in the United States, it is questionable whether this country has actually emphasized parental responsibility in its child support policy. Perhaps more important, parental responsibility and child well-being should both be valued. However, these two virtues are not coherently embodied in the present policy.

The incoherence is illustrated in the history of reform in the public child support system. Although concern about the extent of government intervention partly contributed to the futility of attempts at comprehensive overhaul of the AFDC program, a more central reason for their failure was society's ambivalence about how to balance the adequate financial protection of children and the obligation of the custodial parent to work in the public system of support.[3] As Lawrence Mead argues, the conventional debate on welfare is misdirected. Instead of the customary focus on the *extent* of government intervention, it is the *nature* of government intervention which defines the core of social policy.

Institutional expectations

The nature of government intervention refers to the expectations conveyed to benefit recipients in the program rules and staff attitudes of the program. These are the "operational definition of citizenship."[4] In the case of the traditional AFDC system, the nature of the program is permissive. Program elements from rules to attitudes have failed to send a coherent message of their obligations in return for the public support.

The incremental reforms of AFDC adopted subsequent to the attempted overhaul in Nixon era, on the other hand, reflected a gradual movement toward the recognition of the need to instill expectations, specifically expectations about the work ethic. In this sense the gradual toughening of the work strategy represented a progressive expression of institutional values.

From this perspective, Mead believes the welfare system has emphasized what the government can give but not what the recipients should achieve. The recipients therefore lose sight of their obligation for self-sufficiency, resulting in behavioral dependence by an increasingly large low-income population. Consequently his prescription for reform is neither to increase benefits nor to cut back:

> Welfare is unpopular because it satisfies only half the public mind. To eliminate welfare would satisfy only the other half. The public will remain uncomfortable until a civic version of welfare is realized.[5]

Mead's civic version of welfare is one that instills the "social obligations of citizenship," including the responsibility to work for one's living, to support one's family, to be literate in the English language, to learn enough in school to be employed, and to be a law-abiding citizen.[6] When social programs have rules that clearly convey these institutional expectations to recipients, their behavior will change and welfare dependence and poverty will be reduced through the recipient's own efforts to fulfill their citizenship obligations.

Yet institutional expectations alone are merely a bureaucratic version of family values, too vague to serve as guidelines for policy and too value-laden to stay clear of ideological skirmishes. Even so, Mead's basic premise--mutual reciprocity is essential in social benefit programs--is a sensible starting point for policy design. We will now examine the foundation for mutual reciprocity in child support policy.

Mutual reciprocity

Society has obvious interests in the well-being of children. These interests may stem from altruistic humanitarianism for some and from an economic investment perspective for others. Nonetheless the notion of some type of public responsibility for children, specially children not living with both parents, has never been disputed.[7]

The AFDC program is this country's means of discharging public responsibility. Unfortunately, AFDC was not designed to encourage either parent to take part in the economic support of the child. Until 1984, for instance, payment of private support did not increase a penny the income of a child receiving AFDC since AFDC benefits were reduced dollar-for-dollar by any unearned incomes.[8] In addition, high benefit reduction rate discourages the custodial parent from working. Small wonder why so many noncustodial parents desert their responsibility of paying support and so many custodial parents give up being self-sufficient. The incentive structure is for them to become free riders at the expense of the public.

Edward Gramlich has succinctly conceptualized policy design from a game theory perspective.[9] While his concern is with the fiscal relationship between different levels of government, his analysis can easily be applied to the public child support system. Under his framework of partial utility interdependence, the custodial parent, the noncustodial parent, and the public can be viewed as three parties each concerned only about two types of utility: the party's and the child's. Thus a custodial mother cares about consumption by herself and by her child. If the public is feeding the child anyway and her involvement leads only to corresponding withdrawal of the public with no benefit to the child, it is only rational not to contribute financially. Similar action is easily contemplated by the noncustodial parent under this system.

To maximize joint utility, an alternative model must be designed to create cooperative relationships among the parties. The custodial family's three major sources of income--earnings, private child support, and public child support--may be viewed as a tripartite division of responsibility for supporting children in single-headed families. An adequate policy of child support must assign and affirm responsibilities as well as encourage their fulfillment. In order to have such a policy, two issues, one philosophical and one technical, must be addressed.

The philosophical issue is whether each party--the custodial parent, the noncustodial parent, and the public--

should be expected to discharge their own duty for the child. The consensus in public responsibility for the well-being of poor children has been noted. Now we will briefly sum up the argument for parental responsibilities.

Parental Obligations

In the early 1980s women's participation in the labor force, which had been increasing for the previous three decades, reached a historic milestone: all groups of mothers, including single mothers with young children, have a majority of their members in the labor force.[10] In fact, it is the mothers with young children whose participation rate has increased most dramatically.

This "economic emergence of women"[11] has revolutionized the traditional view of the role of mothers. Specifically it refutes the outdated assumption, underlying the original design of AFDC, that mothers should stay home to take care for their children. As Mead argued, if single mothers not on welfare are working to support their young children, why should those on welfare be expected to do otherwise? Society's normative expectation is strong that custodial parents, most of them mothers, should work to support their own children.

The case is even stronger for the noncustodial parent's obligation for regular support payments. The argument is simple. If parents living with their children are expected to share income with them, there is no reason for noncustodial parents to be treated differently. A noncustodial parent's choice to form a new family certainly does not supersede his or her prior duty.

Organizational Character

The technical issue is how to design the system so as to bring about the mutual reciprocity of responsibility. For this purpose Mead's notion of institutional expectation is too general. A more concrete focus would be the *organizational character* that implements these responsibilities. That is, society should search for the organizational design and provide the organizational resources that would most effectively facilitate the parents in discharging their obligations.

In the successive reforms of the public child support system, for example, the expectation that custodial mothers should work for financial independence was conveyed through incentives and requirements. Yet since the overall structure of the AFDC program continued to discourage work, and since the resources for transition into independence continued to be inadequate, institutional expectations alone had little effect on the problem of welfare dependency.

With respect to noncustodial parent obligations, the standardization of procedures represents a strategy superior to the traditional system of judicial discretion. In the words of Senator Daniel Patrick Moynihan:

> Are there feasible, possibly effective strategies that do commend themselves? Some. One of the arguments put forth in the 1960s in favor of the 'income strategy' to address problems of poverty was the simple administrative fact that the federal government is demonstrably good at redistributing income. Social security retirement benefits are the prime example. From there, it is a small step to the thought that the federal government must also be good at collecting income.[12]

History has shown that the "income strategy" did not succeed in the welfare system, not because of administrative inefficiency, but because of incongruence with the value of parental obligation. Administrative collection of child support, on the other hand, is both efficient and congruent. Collection is but one element of this strategy. The general point is that the entire system of private child support can be upgraded by the government, moving from the traditional discretionary system to a uniform system with standardized procedures applicable universally to every family within the child support system. The public demand is there for the government to move in this direction. As Moynihan further elaborates in referring to the support of babies born out of wedlock:

> This is a matter to be pressed to the point of punitiveness. If the informal sanctions of society will not enforce the principle of legitimacy, let the state do so. Hunt, hound, harass: the absent father is rarely really absent, especially the teenage father, but merely unwilling or not required to acknowledge his children's presence.[13]

To enforce the noncustodial parent's responsibility effectively, one approach is to view it as a tax liability. The entire apparatus of enforcement should be constructed to levy child support as a tax. In a tax model of child support, the standard is uniformly and therefore equitably applied and enforced among all noncustodial parents. In this sense the reform measures undertaken in the last fifteen years have been in the right direction.

But this is only part of the system. The custodial parent's responsibility should also be part of the system of mutual reciprocity. Recent welfare reform efforts have made clear the work ethic expected of custodial parents. Yet the organizational structure of present policy does not sufficiently facilitate work. Instead of replacing earnings as the current public child support system does, public financing of child support should assist custodial parents to obtain employment and to supplement these often meager earnings. To establish the organizational character required for mutual reciprocity, a comprehensive child support policy has to be designed with five essential elements in place.

Elements of Child Support Policy

Private support as tax liability is based upon the proposition that the obligation to one's children is universal. The tax model would also enhance the efficiency of the system. As for public support, supplementation as opposed to replacement of earnings is the only philosophy consistent with the work ethic expected of custodial parents.

This framework of tax liability has five necessary elements: universal establishment of parentage for all children; setting an adequate amount of award through standardized procedures; a mechanism for effective collection of the support owed; supplementation and protection of custodial family income through public financing; and the proper support structure to enable custodial parents to work. There are debatable issues within each element.

Establishing parentage

Divorce or nonmarital birth place a child in the eligibility pool, but it does not become part of the private child support system unless and until a child support award is established. This step is especially difficult for never-married mothers when paternity has not been legally established. In 1990, fewer than a quarter of unwed mothers had a child support order. In contrast, almost eight out of every ten divorced mothers did.[14]

Establishing an award, however, is part of what one might call a broader "parentage establishment policy." Parentage establishment confers upon the parent both obligations and rights. In order to establish an award, the noncustodial parent must be identified, located, and parentage must be officially adjudicated.[15]

A comprehensive child support policy would institutionalize an efficient mechanism to have these procedures carried out for all children. These procedures would ensure the obligations of parentage. Just as important are procedures delineating the rights of parentage, including visitation and a decision-making role in the child's life. Parentage rights must also be part of this policy.

Until two decades age, not every state was willing to guarantee the right to paternal support of children born out of wedlock. The change only came about after a series of Supreme Court decisions in the late 1960s.[16] Since then, a network of parent locator services has emerged to help search for noncustodial parents. Paternity is adjudicated in court. Custodial parents receiving welfare run the risk of losing part of the benefits if they do not assist in this process.

To opponents of mandatory paternity establishment, requiring custodial mothers receiving public child support to aid in the search of the child's father is tantamount to harassment. Some custodial parents may wish to sever all ties to the noncustodial parents. Others feel that unmarried motherhood is stigmatized through such a process. Another objection to the emphasis on pursuing paternity is its cost effectiveness. Locating fathers and establishing paternity can be costly, but expected collections are low because unwed fathers tend to have lower than average income.

A rebuttal to the cost effectiveness argument is that rigorous pursuit of paternity has a deterrence effect on irresponsible parents. Moreover, it is not clear that paternity determination action is not cost effective today, as the accuracy of blood tests has improved and the costs have decreased.[17] Research also indicates that the incomes of these noncustodial parents, if low at all, may be just temporarily so. A study of court records and tax returns in Wisconsin shows that the personal income of noncustodial fathers whose children were on AFDC had increased by one-half over a seven-year period.[18]

Finally, as child support is seen in light of the tax model, the responsibility of the noncustodial parent to the child and to the public should be given higher priority than the custodial parent's potential privacy interests of not establishing paternity.[19] In fact, the current policy has in a way already adopted the tax model where public child support is involved, since participation in paternity identification is mandatory if the custodial parent is a beneficiary of government support. The problem of this approach is that targeting the requirement adds to its stigma.

If the tax liability model is extended to all families, the requirement for parentage establishment would apply to all out-of-wedlock births regardless of economic status or welfare recipiency. An exemption ought to be available to individuals in hardship cases such as rape. This tax liability model would enforce the principle of parental responsibility to its full extent. It also expands the non-marital child's rights beyond support payments to rights in inheritance, social insurance entitlement, and family identity.[20]

The Family Support Act requires the mother to provide the social security numbers of both parents at the birth of a child. Most Western European countries have a national registry of their populations.[21] That explains why paternity adjudication is not an issue even in Scandinavian countries where the out-of-wedlock birth rate is comparable to that in the United States. The size and heterogeneity of this country would probably render a national registry less effective than its counterparts in Europe, but the real barrier lies in our cultural resistance to such a mechanism. The parental social security number reporting requirement is thus a small but significant first step in developing this much needed system of identification and location of noncustodial parents.

Mutual reciprocity requires not only the imposition of parental obligations, but also the acknowledgement of parental rights.[22] One of the most obvious rights of noncustodial parents is the right to have contacts with their children. In fact, visitation and access to children have become one of the most contentious issues in child support. Some custodial parents feel they have a right to refuse visitation when the noncustodial parent is delinquent in their payments, while many noncustodial parents feel they have no obligation to provide for the children whom they do not get to see.

As intuitive as these arguments sound, one ought to realize that the child's right to financial support is distinct from the noncustodial parent's right to access, and the policy to separate these issues should continue. At the same time, noncustodial parents who keep in contact with their children tend to do better in paying child support.[23] Both because of this empirical relationship and because of the noncustodial parent's rights, visitation should be sanctioned as part of the overall arrangements.

There seem to be two necessary steps in the public's sanction. At the policy level, the system should have standard guidelines on non-financial penalties for non-compliance. Under this scheme, no custodial parents--other than those exempted by courts--would be allowed to refuse visitation by forfeiting their child support awards. In reciprocity, no noncustodial parents should be able to voluntarily trade their right of access to the child for the forgiveness of support obligations. At the individual level, however, it must be recognized that the interpersonal dimension is the most important element in fostering mutual reciprocity between the parties involved in a family disruption. Therefore counseling and mediation processes are essential as well.[24]

Setting award

The second necessary element in a comprehensive child support system is a normative standard to determine the amount of support owed. Congress has required states to devise numeric guidelines that are rebuttably presumptive for this purpose. Is this a sound policy?

There are two major arguments in favor of setting obligations through a legislative numeric formula. First, the public has a direct financial stake in the amount of payment by noncustodial parents whose children receive public money, so the apportionment of support between the two parents and the public is in a sense a political issue best resolved through the legislative rather than judicial channels. Second, the traditional discretionary approach depends too much upon the attitudes of the local magistrates, the bargaining power of the ex-spouses and the skills of their attorneys. Like cases are rarely treated alike under such an approach.

In contrast, the traditional argument for the reliance on the judicial process is that each case is unique. Some children may better benefit from in-kind support or property from the noncustodial parent. Courts are better suited for such a task. Moreover, it may be argued that most divorcing parents reach agreements without judicial intervention, and most of the arguments for a legislative formula for the amount of child support would therefore be satisfied by guidelines rather than presumptive standards.

At issue is the extent to which the determination of the amount of child support should be transformed from judicial discretion to a resemblance of the system of taxation. The arguments in favor of judicial discretion have ignored the realties of the judicial system. When the number of broken marriages and paternity cases is small, greater equity is achieved by tailoring agreements to each case. This was probably true at some point in the past, when judges could consider every minute detail of all relevant circumstances. Justice was better served tailoring the award to each individual case. But when the number of cases is large and the system inevitably becomes more impersonal, the argument in favor of individualization breaks down. Instead, standardization becomes a more equitable treatment under most situations.

To push the tax liability model to the extreme, the entry of a standardized award amount may be made an automatic process triggered administratively by a divorce decree or paternity adjudication; any rebuttal to the presumed amount would be initiated through a separate administrative or judicial review process. The limitation of such a procedure is that it does not address issues like custody and visitation which are intimately linked to support obligations. As long as the standards are not developed to take into account these issues, such a system is bound to be bogged down by the high incidence of appeals. For the present, making the pre-set amount of child support award a rebuttable presumption does seem to be a reasonable compromise.

Another issue in determining the amount of the award is its adjustment over time. Traditionally, states have no established administrative procedures to revise child support orders over time. Typically a judicial process must be initiated by either parent who desires an adjustment in the amount of award. The adoption of the tax liability model suggests a routine mechanism for updating award. An administrative route would make periodic review available to all child support cases at low cost. While the Family Support Act establishes the mandate for periodic review, it contains no guidelines on implementation.

To some advocates of the traditional system, freezing the award level is proper. Since the noncustodial parent no longer lives with the child, their attachment weakens over time; and the decrease in real value of the support award only accurately reflects this disengagement.

Moreover, automatic updating of a support award tends to distort work behavior. If the award is indexed to the earnings of the noncustodial parent, it results in a higher marginal tax rate for him or her. If the award is a function of the incomes of both the custodial and noncustodial parents, there is an incentive to reduce one's own share before the mandatory review of the award. Under the traditional system, these distortions are minimized because of the sporadic and uncertain nature of updating through litigations.

Yet parental obligation should not be shunned because of separate residence or lapse of time. The traditional process is ineffective in upholding this obligation over time, and a more efficient administrative mechanism is needed to prevent child support from being eroded by inflation. The practical procedures for setting up this mechanism is one of the most critical issues in child support enforcement, to be pursued in the next chapter.

Collecting support

The collection of support is another essential element in a comprehensive child support system. Without improvement in the collection mechanism, perfecting the determination of award would be meaningless. At least two issues are relevant at the collection stage: the mechanism of collection and the agency overseeing such a mechanism.

In several steps, Congress has embraced wage withholding as a widely applicable mechanism for child support collection. Withholding upon delinquency was required in the 1984 amendment. Then, in 1988 universal and immediate withholding on all new cases was passed, effective in 1990 for cases receiving IV-D services and in 1994 for all other cases.

Immediate withholding of income in all cases may be construed as an invasion of privacy. By replacing personal touch with bureaucratic procedures, it also prevents non-custodial parents from participating actively in supporting their offsprings. Moreover, employers have to bear an extra administrative burden.

Each of these criticisms also applies to withholding upon delinquency, except that, in the latter cases, the noncustodial parent may be seen as deserving the punishment because of non-payment. However, in a taxation model, immediate withholding is routinized and the element of punishment and stigma is to a large extent removed.

The strongest argument in favor of the tax model is that taxing at source is far more effective than collection upon default. If there is a consensus that the support of one's child is a paramount obligation, guaranteeing its fulfillment by universal automatic withholding does not seem to be a radical measure. To the children, the ensuing regularity and stability of payments provide security in every sense of that word. The best interest of the child therefore should in most cases override the potential preference of the noncustodial parent for privacy.

Such a measure is also necessary given the empirical evidence. In the traditional system, 70 percent of all noncustodial parents have been delinquent in their support payment at some point within a three year period.[25] Uniform automatic withholding then only renders the system more efficient and convenient than the alternative process triggered by non-payment. A study of various Wisconsin counties indicates that, even at the early stage of implementation, universal immediate withholding leads to an increase in collections between 11 and 30 percent.[26] This is one area where the model of taxation should be applied for all its advantages.

With automatic wage withholding as the mechanism for collection, the second issue is who should be in charge for such a mechanism. The problem in the traditional system stems from the difficulty in monitoring what are most of the time private and informal nature of the payment arrangements. Some states have long mandated payment through the court but compliance is generally low, and the judicial system does not have sufficient resources to enforce the payments. Only in 1975 had the federal government begun to require welfare recipients to assign child support rights to the state office of child support, thus establishing the state IV-D agencies as the official channel of payments for noncustodial parents in welfare cases. These agencies have now expanded their role to cover non-welfare families requesting services voluntarily.

The expansion of service to non-welfare families is indicative of the trend to make the collection of support more similar to the collection of taxes. Opponents to this trend generally see it as bureaucratic encroachment into private lives. There is also the belief that efficiency is compromised by setting up government intermediaries. Furthermore, the direct payment of support may be useful in some cases as a way to maintain contacts between the parents, as well as between the absent parent and the child.

The empirical fact, however, is that many noncustodial parents do not keep up with their payment. And as the number of child support cases increases, the court is no longer capable of monitoring payment. The introduction of a public administrative agency therefore increases efficiency, not decreases it. Given the burden of collecting from so many cases, the uniform collection from all non-custodial parents through an administrative unit seems not only logical but necessary.

Public financial protection

The fourth element in a comprehensive child support system is the government's role in paying support benefits. This need arises because many noncustodial parents simply do not have the resources to pay for an adequate level of sustenance for their children. Also, there are bound to be some uncollectible awards and slippage in private support even in the best enforcement system.

The current public support system provides a means-tested minimum benefit. Since the AFDC program limits eligibility to the poor, it penalizes earnings and is not conducive to the enforcement of the custodial parent's responsibility to earn to support the children. Nor does the program protect the non-poor from irregular private support payments.

Much needed is a program of public benefits that supplements rather than replaces earnings. A minimum benefit can improve the economic status of some of the custodial parents and their children. Combined with earnings, this benefit may also lift many single-parent households out of poverty. Income security is another justification for a guaranteed benefit. It reduces the risk to children whose noncustodial parents have become unemployed or unable to work. In such cases, child support income falls, if at all, to the guaranteed level, not to zero.

As discussed in the last chapter, a consensus is emerging regarding the reform of the public child support system. This consensus focuses on the value of self-suffi-ciency but not necessarily on the specific strategies. How a scheme of public financial protection can be implement-ed is the subject of chapter 5.

Support infrastructure

In order for custodial parents to discharge their financial responsibility to their own children and be the primary caretaker at the same time, society as a whole must be willing to share some of their burden. Thus a system of child support should include an adequate support structure for work.

This support structure should include several parts. First, assistance in seeking employment should be available. Workfare demonstration projects illustrate that when welfare families are offered sufficient help, some can work their way out of welfare.[27] In New York City's Project Redirection, even the group deemed least able to benefit from services--teenage mothers on welfare--prove responsive to skills training and job search services.[28]

Unfortunately, securing employment is not in itself equivalent to better economic well-beings. Evidence shows that while workfare projects are successful in moving some families off welfare, those families themselves tend to remain in poverty.[29] This is partly due to their low market wage rate. Even when the market wage of these custodial families is comparable to that of two-parent families, there still is a case for additional government support. Given housework and child care, the net earnings capacity of a single parent is necessarily lower than that of a married couple. Indeed, child care has been singled out as the major impediment to maternal employment, whether they are on public assistance or not.[30] Child care is prominent on the policy agenda of many industrialized countries, it must also be part of a system of child support that seeks to encourage self-sufficiency.

The final major component in an adequate support structure is health insurance. The coupling of AFDC and Medicaid creates a strong incentive for welfare families to remain dependent on the program for fear of losing their medical assistance. Since many single parents can be expected to work in low-paying or part-time jobs, health insurance is not generally available as part of their compensation package. Research conducted since the Omnibus Budget Reconciliation Act of 1981 terminated the AFDC eligibility of many families shows that health care is a most significant issue for these families.[31] To encourage work by custodial parents, some form of publicly supported medical insurance arrangement must be in place.

Enforcement versus Financing

This chapter has identified five important dimensions for a comprehensive child support policy. The first three dimensions--parentage establishment, award determination, and support collections--pertain to the enforcement of private child support. The last two elements require public financing--a program to guarantee minimum support level, and the development of a network of services to facilitate parental employment.

In order to uphold the triangle of responsibilities--from the noncustodial parent, the custodial parent, and society--toward children, child support policy must create an organizational structure conducive to the enforcement of these responsibilities. The tax liability model of child support enforcement enhances the likelihood of compliance by the noncustodial parent. Therefore the bureaucratic administration and standardized procedures are sound foundation for further policy development.

While recent reforms have moved in this direction, the coverage of bureaucratic enforcement continues to be defined in terms of recipiency status in publicly financed child support. Participation in IV-D is mandatory for families receiving AFDC, but voluntary for others. This distinction places a severe limit on the concept of child support as tax liability. It implies that parental liability is conditional.

Nor has the public financing of child support fulfilled the public obligations set forth in our framework. Further revision of the child support system should address both these issues.

Notes for Chapter 3

1. Blanche Bernstein, *The Politics of Welfare: The New York City Experience* (Cambridge MA: Abt Books, 1982) p. 64.

2. Alfred J. Kahn and Sheila B. Kamerman, eds., *From Data Collection to Social Policy* (Newbury Park CA: Sage, 1988).

3. Lawrence Mead, *Beyond Entitlement: The Social Obligation of Citizenship* (New York NY: Free Press, 1985), pp.102-111.

4. *Ibid.*, p. 7.

5. *Ibid.*, p. 236.

6. *Ibid.*, p. 242.

7. The specific expression of this interest has of course varied with time, but the significant point is that the idea of public intervention for these children has existed throughout American history. For variations of this idea in the United States, see Grace Abbott, *The Child and the State* (Chicago: University of Chicago Press, 1938) and Robert H. Bremner, *Children and Youth in America: A Documentary History* (Cambridge MA: Harvard University Press, 1970).

8. As discussed in Chapter 2, a $50 set-aside provision was created in the 1984 Amendment.

9. Edward M. Gramlich, "Cooperation and Competition in Public Welfare Policies," *Journal of Policy Analysis and Management* 6 (1987): 417-431.

10. Susan E. Shank, "Women and the Labor Market: The Link Grows Stronger," *Monthly Labor Review* 111 (3) (1988): 3-8.

11. Barbara R. Bergmann, *The Economic Emergence of Women* (New York NY: Free Press, 1985).

12. Daniel Patrick Moynihan, *Family and Nation* (New York: Harcourt Brace and Javonovich, 1986) p. 179.

13. *Ibid.*, p. 180.

14. U.S Bureau of the Census, Current Population Report, Child Support and Alimony, (1989), Series P-60, No. 173.

15. For a description of the process, see Sandra K. Danziger and Ann Nichols-Casebelt, "Child Support in Paternity Cases," *Social Service Review* 64 (1990): 458-474.

16. Harry D. Krause, "The Uniform Parentage Act," *Family Law Quarterly* 8 (1974): 1-16.

17. Currently the maximum cost for positive identification of paternity is about $400 in genetic tests, but in most cases the tests involved are considerably less expensive. See Chapter 6 of Michael R. Henry and Victoria S. Schwartz, *A Guide for Judges in Child Support Enforcement*, 2nd ed. (Chevy Chase MD: U.S. Department of Health and Human Services, Office of Child Support Enforcement 1987).

18. Elizabeth Phillips and Irwin Garfinkel, *Changes Over Time in the Incomes of Nonresident Fathers in Wisconsin* (Madison WI: Institute for Research on Poverty, Discussion Paper 967, 1987)

19. The Uniform Illegitimacy Act, approved by the Conference of Commissioners on Uniform State Laws in 1922, sided with the privacy interests of the mother and recommended that no paternity proceedings be initiated over the objection of a mother who was not financially dependent on the state. This is the basis of most state statutes today. In contrast, the Children's Bureau back then took the view that public authority should have the right to establish paternity whenever in the interest of the child. See Marigold S Melli, *Child Support: A Survey of the States*. (Madison, WI: University of Wisconsin Institute for Research on Poverty Special Report, 1984).

20. Esther Wattenberg, "Establishment of Paternity for Nonmarital Children: Do Policy and Practice Discourage Adjudication?" *Public Welfare* 3 (1987): 8-13.

21. Irwin Garfinkel and Pat Wong, "Child Support and Public Policy," in *Lone-parent Families: The Economic Challenge* (Paris: Organization for Economic Cooperation and Development, 1990).

22. Marigold S. Melli, "The Changing Legal Status of the Single Parent" *Family Relations* 35 (1986):31-35.

23. Frank F. Furstenberg, Jr., "Marital Disruption, Child Custody, and Visitation" in Alfred J. Kahn and Sheila B. Kamerman, eds., *Child Support: From Debt Collection to Social Policy* (Beverley Hills, CA: Sage Publications, 1988). Judith A. Seltzer, Nora Cate Shaeffer, and Hong-Wen Charng, "Family Ties after Divorce: The Relationship between Visitation and Paying Child Support," *Journal of Marriage and the Family*, 51 (1989): 1013-1031.

24. Susan Myers, Geoff Gallas, Roger Hanson, and Susan Keilitz, "Court-Sponsored Mediation of Divorce, Custody, Visitation, and Support" *State Court Journal* (1989): 24-31.

25. This conclusion is obtained from examining a sample of court records in 20 counties in Wisconsin.

26. Irwin Garfinkel and Marieka Klawitter, "The Effect of Routine Income Withholding on Child Support Collection," *Journal of Policy Analysis and Management* 9 (1990): 155-177.

27. Judith M. Gueron and Edward Pauly, *From Welfare to Work* (New York NY: Russell Sage Foundation, 1991).

28. Barbara B. Blum, "Helping Teenage Mothers," *Public Welfare* 42 (1984): 17-22.

29. David T. Ellwood, *Poor Support* (New York NY: Norton, 1986).

30. Barbara R. Bergmann, *The Economic Emergence of Women* (New York NY: Free Press, 1985).

31. I. Moscovice and G. Davidson, "Health Care and Insurance Loss of Working AFDC Recipients," *Medical Care* 25 (1987): 413-425.

4

Issues in Private Support Enforcement

This country has made a lot of progress in exerting administrative control over the enforcement of private child support. Yet in 1991, the National Commission on Children offered the following evaluation: "Current state systems for child support enforcement are inadequate at every step--from the establishment of child support awards to the collection of payments. The federal system of support and guidance to the states is also inadequate."[1] This assessment is reflected in the average grade of C- that state child support enforcement programs gave the federal OCSE operation, and the similarly low ratings the federal government awarded state programs.[2]

Part of the reason for the pessimism is undoubtedly the insufficient amount of time allowed for system development. Policy implementation takes time, as does institutional learning. Yet the public in general, and politicians in particular, are often impatient to see the result of reform.[3] The last two major rounds of welfare reform were separated by merely four years. By 1990 some states were still struggling to let the earlier reform measures sink in, let alone the barrage of changes required by the 1988 legislation. The system is still in the process of muddling through a very unstable environment, and it is perhaps too soon to pronounce welfare reform a failure.

Assessment of Reform in Enforcement

In fact, program statistics on private child support enforcement indicate that some progress has been made in the last decade. As Table 4.1 shows, for the nation's IV-D programs as a whole, performance indicators on collections, parent location, paternity establishment, and award establishment have all moved in upward trends, with improvements ranging from 165 percent over twelve years in amount collected to 258 percent in parents located. These numbers indicate that IV-D programs are expanding their role and are serving more custodial families.

Unfortunately, the expansion of Title IV-D has not translated into better outcome for the entire population of potentially child-support-eligible families. The bottom panel of Table 4.1 reports results from national sample surveys of the entire child-support-eligible population carried out periodically.[4] The results from the Census Bureau surveys indicate that the proportion of the population who have an award and the proportion who receive some payment have hardly increased during this period. The only positive sign comes from total collections. The small increase towards the end of the 1980s is consistent with what can be expected of the various collections techniques, from income withholding to tax intercept, that were gradually adopted at the state level in the early part of the decade.

Taken together, the program statistics and survey results indicate that the increase in IV-D services cannot keep pace with the increase in the national pool of families eligible for child support. Between 1979 and 1990, the number of mothers in this pool increased from 7.1 million to 10 million. More importantly, within this population the number of never-married mothers more than doubled from 1.4 million to 3 million. Since unmarried mothers face the most barriers in the private child support system, there is little surprise that the national picture on award establishment did not improve.

Possibly as a result, the two indicators on overall performance of IV-D programs have stayed stagnant over the past few years. AFDC recovery ratio inched upward to 10.5 percent in 1991, while the ratio of collections to

Table 4.1

Child Support Enforcement Statistics
Comparison of IV-D and Census Data
1978-1989

Measure	1978	1983	1985	1987	1989	Percent change, 1978-89
From IV-D program statistics:						
Total collections[a] (billions)	$2.0	$2.5	$3.1	$4.3	$5.3	165
Parents located (thousands)	454	831	878	1,145	1,624	258
Paternits established (thousands)	111	208	232	269	339	205
Awards established (thousands)	315	496	669	812	936	197
Percent AFDC payments recovered	([b])	6.6	7.3	9.1	10.0	([b])
Total collections per $ of administrative costs	$3.35	$2.93	$3.31	$3.68	$3.85	149
From Census Surveys:						
Total collections (billions)[a]	$8.9	$8.8	$8.3	$10.9	$11.2	26
IV-D collections as percent of total collections	23	28	37	39	47	104
Of demographically eligible, percent with awards	59	58	61	59	58	-2
Of demographically eligible, percent who received some payment	35	35	37	39	37	6

[a] Constant (1989) dollars using Consumer Price Index.
[b] Not available.

Source: U.S. House of Representatives, *Overview of Entitlement Programs: 1992 Green Book.* Washington, DC: Governmetn Printing Office. 1992, pp. 708-709.

expenditures fluctuated around $3.8 on a dollar for the last few years.

Thus there are two plausible theories for the present lack of improvement in outcome. The first is the bureaucracy's need to adjust to the numerous changes required by federal mandates. If this is the case, the passage of time is the solution, and there is little policymakers can or should do.

If, on the other hand, the effectiveness of the enforcement mechanism is hampered by "extraneous" events or by the behavior of the individuals in the target population, then a more pro-active approach should be adopted. For in the design and implementation of policy, no events are completely extraneous. The enforcement bureaucracy should be made more responsive to these events instead. The increasing proportion of births that are nonmarital is one such event. The frequent interstate mobility of former coupes is another example.

Econometric evidence shows that the enforcement bureaucracy kept private support collections from declining as a result of the demographic changes over time.[5] At the same time, there are features in this bureaucratic structure that make responsiveness to some critical problems difficult. We will examine some of these problems according to the three elements on private child support in the normative framework identified in the last chapter.[6]

Paternity Determination

Paternity establishment remains the weakest link in the enforcement system, a "step child" in policy development.[7] In 1989, the nationwide ratio between the annual number of paternities established by IV-D and the total number of nonmarital births was 31 percent.[8] Although this is substantial improvement over the 19 percent ten years before, it is still a low success rate.

In addition, children born out of wedlock, for whom paternity determination is the first and most difficult hurdle before obtaining a child support award, account for an increasingly larger share of the child-support-eligible population. The current pool of unmarried women with children below eighteen is 3 million. Yet in 1991 there were 1.1 million nonmarital births in this country, up 25 percent from just four years ago. At this rate the pool will expand very rapidly even though some of the nonmarried births will be legitimated through subsequent marriage of the parents.[9] If paternity determination for this fastest-growing subgroup does not substantially improve, it will be difficult to imagine future improvements in the total number of custodial families with an award.

State child support enforcement agencies have been required to pursue paternity for AFDC cases since 1967. Subsequent legislation has also relaxed the statutes of limitation on paternity actions to the 18th birthday of the child. However, the structure of the child support enforcement system itself does not encourage these efforts.

Misdirected organizational incentives

The first impediment is the structure of federal incentive payments. States have always been allowed to retain a portion of the federal government's share of private support collected from noncustodial parents. These incentives are now set at between 6 and 10 percent of total private collections from both AFDC cases and non-AFDC cases. The higher the cost-effectiveness of the state program, measured by the dollar amount of collections per dollar of administrative costs,[10] the larger the percentage rate.

The problem with this incentives structure is that it penalizes vigorous attempts to pursue paternity cases. Relative to other IV-D program activities, paternity determination is probably the most labor-intensive task. In 1987, the average paternity determination case cost $910 which did not include expenses on award establishment and collection.[11] On the revenue side, the amount of the award is likely to be small since putative fathers tend to have lower income. It is also harder to collect from after an award is established. The average payment received by never-married custodial mothers, to whom practically all paternity determination action could be attributed, was $1,888 in 1989. The average amount received by divorced mothers for the same year was $3,322.[12] The lower payment to never-married mothers may be partly due to the typically smaller number of children in this group. Nonetheless, from the perspective of bureaucratic incentives, the reward for pursuing paternity in nonmarital cases is low.

Evidence shows that state agencies do indeed give paternity adjudication very low priority.[13] The General Accounting Office in its review of state programs came to this conclusion as it discusses the effect of incentive payments on paternity establishment:

> Staff resources were directed toward cases with the greatest apparent collection potential and away from those cases that appeared to require greater development effort, such as those needing paternity determinations. Thus, they denied children the social benefits resulting from determining paternity.[14]

Another impediment to paternity establishment is the decidedly adversarial nature of the procedures in many state. While administrative bureaucracy has been set up to address other dimensions of private support enforcement, paternity proceedings in many jurisdictions have retained the traditional posture of legal actions against bastardy. In some states, such as Oklahoma, even if a father wishes to acknowledge paternity voluntarily, he is still required to go through a court proceeding to establish paternity.

The heavy involvement of the courts in paternity determination can be partly traced to the antiquated concept of "illegitimacy." The pseudo-criminal nature of the procedures discourages parental responsibility by making it difficult for unwed fathers to acknowledge their relationship to the child. The recent report by the U.S. Commission on Interstate Child Support also stated that "criminalizing nonmarital parentage hinders civil parentage determinations."[15] In short, the current system has the effect of penalizing nonmarital children through the stigmatization of the parentage establishment process.

If the policy objective is to honor marriage as an institution, it can be accomplished by conferring additional privileges on married couples instead. The State of Wisconsin has adopted this approach of encouraging marriage among teenage unwed parents. *Married* teenage couples in Wisconsin are eligible to enroll in a special version of the AFDC program that allows them to keep a significant amount of their earnings while they are completing high-school.

The personal dimension

Some of the resistance to paternity establishment comes from the mothers themselves. A demonstration project in Ohio found that expedited procedures in paternity establishment succeeded in increasing the number of voluntary acknowledgement, but 45 percent of the custodial mothers for whom expedited procedures were available (experimental group) either did not show up for their initial interview, or refused to cooperate in the process at a later stage. This was the same percentage of non-cooperation as in the control group.[16]

There are two likely reasons for such findings. First, some single mothers consciously wish to avoid establishing paternity. Wattenberg found that many teenage mothers did so for "the long-term interests of their male partners, hoping that by not pursuing paternity identification, they would protect their partners from financial consequences, harassment, medical expenses, prison, and even statutory rape charges."[17]

As discussed in the last chapter, however, this cannot be a valid argument. If the best interest of the child is to

be the guiding principle, parentage ought to be established
in all cases with the possible exception of rape and incest,
even if it sometimes infringes upon the interests of either
or both parents. Moreover, the teenage custodial mothers
themselves often regret not having established paternity a
few years later, as they observe the changes in economic
circumstances over time, often in opposite directions,
between their partners and themselves.[18]

The other possible reason for the lack of cooperation
among unmarried mothers in paternity determination is
that they perceive the procedure, even though expedited,
as cumbersome. If at the time they do not perceive the
need of establishing paternity as immediate and important
enough to warrant going through these procedures, they
may simply ignore the system. If that is the case, there is
certainly a strong argument for instituting a uniform and
routine process of paternity establishment at a low time-
cost to the custodial mothers and preferably early on in
their parenthood.

Procedural solutions

The most effective solution to the problem of
parentage establishment appears to be the adoption of
universal procedures of acknowledgement at childbirth.
The reporting of parents' social security numbers required
by the Family Support Act is one step in this direction.

Another mechanism, pioneered by the State of
Washington, is to have a voluntary paternity acknowledgement procedure at childbirth. Under the Uniform Parentage Code adopted by that state, hospitals are required to
offer the opportunity for paternity establishment to
unmarried fathers at the hospital. Parentage can be
established right then and there if the unmarried father
signs an affidavit acknowledging fatherhood. Hospitals
are reimbursed a $20 fee per case for this responsibility.

Many states are in the process of passing legislation
to confer upon voluntary acknowledgement of paternity

the same legal effect as court adjudication. The hospital-based approach seems to represent the most routinized, low-cost, and pro-active method. The success rate is also high as few fathers would turn down the offer at their proudest moment.

To address unwed mothers' avoidance of paternity establishment, the proper long-term strategy is to educate young parents about the importance of parentage establishment. Some states have developed comprehensive parental responsibility curricula, addressing the legal, social, and financial ramifications of parenthood. Georgia, for example, publishes a newspaper, called *Looking Beyond Teenage Pregnancy*, with teenagers as its target readers. The publication explores issues such as parental responsibility and child support.

Both the establishment of simple administrative procedures for paternity acknowledgement and the education and information campaigns are consistent with the tax liability model of child support. The former simplifies and standardizes procedures to make compliance as painless as possible, and the latter raises the consciousness of citizenship by making voluntary compliance a natural and honorable responsibility.

Award Review and Adjustment

The second element in a comprehensive child support policy involves the determination of the size of the award. With the requirement in the Family Support Act to adopt state formulas as rebuttable presumptions for award adjudications, the issue of setting the initial award has been settled.

An unsettled and less apparent issue is the adjustment of an award over time. There is plenty of empirical evidence documenting the need for periodic adjustment in obligations. A review of court cases in Wisconsin shows that, on the average, the initial amount of award conforms closely with state guidelines expressed as a percentage of

the noncustodial parent's income. Over time, however, few
awards are increased to catch up with the income increase
of the noncustodial parents, and the adequacy of support
is gradually eroded by inflation.[19] Research based on
national data likewise indicates that erosion of award
accounts for up to half of the discrepancy between actual
award levels and the widely adopted normative standards.[20]

The Family Support Act requires periodic review and
adjustment every three years. Initial results of demonstration projects show that this review process is time consum-
ing even when the modification is through stipulation or
mediation. Adjustments made through the court is, of
course, even more of a laborious process.[21]

If we are to follow a tax liability approach, the
revision and adjustment process, like paternity determination, should be an administrative one that requires as little
time and effort as possible. The feasibility of this depends
largely on the factors included in the standard itself. The
simpler a formula for determining the award, the easier
will be the application of automated technology for its
adjustment.

Automated solution

At the most basic level, initial award standards could
be accompanied by a provision on automatic revision. If
the revision is indexed only to price level (adjustment to
inflation), it can be carried out simply with an automated
registry of all child support cases.

One of the merits of price-indexing of an award is
that it provides a steady level of private support since the
child's entitlement would be constant in real value. It is
also consistent with the notion of absent parent disengagement since the level of parental responsibility is frozen at
the real value of the initial award. The child would not
have a stake in the subsequent improvement or deteriora-
tion in the noncustodial parent's living standard. A

practical problem of price-indexing is whether the parent can still afford to pay in the event of a subsequent reduction in income. Also, in view of the fact that many young fathers with low income have substantial increase in their earnings over time, this approach would not be tapping the full potential of noncustodial parents to support their children.

Even if other factors are included in the formula for review and adjustment, it is still possible to have an automated adjustment process if all the information required is included in the automated registry, and, equally important, if a mechanism is available for the periodic update of the registry. This registry would electronically compute the new child support liabilities at the end of each period under the triennial review required by current legislation. The parties involved would receive mailed notifications of the revised amount of the award. Much like the process of property tax assessment, unless the results are appealed, there would be no need for a modification hearing at all. It would be far less costly, in terms of both time and money, than a system that mandates a hearing in every single case. The means of setting up this automated process will be addressed in greater detail after we have examined the issue of collection.

Collecting Support

The Family Support Act requires the universal application of immediate wage withholding for all new child support orders by 1994. With administrative procedures implemented under federal guidelines, this mechanism is effective during the initial establishment of order. In order for withholding to be truly effective, however, the system must be equipped to address two subsequent issues. The first has to do with changes in the employment of noncustodial parents. The second is the problem of interstate collection.

There are frequent job turnovers among some noncustodial parents. One study shows that a high percentage of immediate income withholding orders are terminated within six months: 40 percent among noncustodial parents whose children are on AFDC and 28 percent among those whose children are not.[22] While employers are required by law to report the termination of employment of noncustodial parents with a withholding order, reporting is often done on a monthly or quarterly basis to the state employment service agency only. By the time this information is channeled back to the IV-D agency, some noncustodial parents may have already moved on to a third job.

The State of Washington recently carried out an employer reporting program demonstration to address the issue of job turnover. Employers in five industries, including building and construction which typically have higher than average worker turnover, are required under the program to report information on new employees directly to the state child support enforcement agency within 35 days of the employment. The enforcement agency maintains an information registry on all IV-D cases. If the names of the new employees submitted by employers match those with support obligations, a new withholding order is issued immediately. In the first 18 months of its implementation, the program succeeded in collecting from 43 percent of newly-hired noncustodial parents in the demonstration project who had owed child support in the previous year, at a cost effectiveness ratio of $22 collected on each dollar of program cost.[23]

The experience of this program points to the importance of integrating the collection mechanism with the entire employment reporting system. Since existing regulations already require timely reporting of employees for tax purposes, coupling the child support enforcement function with the employment system would reduce the time lag observed in the traditional reporting system at little additional cost to the employer.

Interstate child support collection is another weakness of the current enforcement apparatus. A review by the General Accounting Office shows that procedures for serving out-of-state wage withholding orders are hardly uniform, and that the response time between the initial order and the actual collection takes much longer than in intrastate cases.[24]

Interstate relocations of noncustodial parents are not at all uncommon. A study indicates that a year after the break-up, 12 percent of the former couples live in different states. That percentage rises to 25 percent in three years, and 40 percent eight years after the break-up.[25] At this rate of mobility overtime, the inefficiency of interstate collection becomes equivalent to inefficiency of overall collection. Coupled with the problem of employment instability, the problem of interstate collection threatens to undermine the automatic withholding mechanism.

Organizational solution

The inefficiency of interstate collection stems from the need to go through multiple bureaucracies operating under procedures of different states. The tax liability model would dictate the unifying of withholding procedures by delegating the task to a singular entity, in the same way that it would be advisable to remove the state employment service as the intermediary of new-employee reporting.

To break down jurisdictional barriers, the organizational entity best suited for this collection function should be at the federal level. Solving both the employment reporting problem and the interstate collection problem requires separating the task of wage withholding from state IV-D agencies. Instead, this task should be delegated to a new federal agency with direct access to federal employment-based information systems would be.

Two possibilities for such an agency are the Internal Revenue Service (IRS) and the Social Security Administration (SSA). In fact, the new agency may be created as divisions within the IRS or the SSA to carry out the wage withholding function for child support collection. Alternatively, the federal Office of Child Support Enforcement may establish a withholding division with a working agreement with either or both IRS and SSA.

The Commission on Interstate Child Support has considered the possibility of moving the entire OCSE to the IRS but has declined to make such a recommendation.[26] Part of the concern is the IRS's lack of experience in child support enforcement functions other than collections. The proposal here is much narrower. Moving only the routine collection function to the IRS would take advantage of the strength of the IRS in collection without sacrificing efficiency in other child support functions.

Regardless of whether this new agency will be set up as part of the IRS or the current federal Office of Child Support Enforcement, we will refer to it as the federal Child Support Collection Division (CSCD). This proposed agency would operate a national child support registry. When an award is established and a wage withholding order initiated by a state court or IV-D agency, it is fed into the registry at CSCD. Since the registry is linked with the federal employment data system, the support obligation and withholding order become an integral part of the IRS file or the social security record of each noncustodial parent in the labor force. CSCD would serve the withholding order on the current employer of the noncustodial parent. When there is a change in employment, the new employment information submitted to the IRS or the SSA would trigger the support order, and the new employer will be notified of the need to withhold wages as well.

This system would ensure that the support order follows the individual worker as he or she changes jobs or residency within the United States. The process of collection by withholding would therefore be far more manageable than the existing system. The withheld amount would be sent by the employers to the CSCD, which could send the monthly private support payment to the custodial families directly. If a decentralized disbursement mechanism is desired, the child support collected could also be transferred back to state IV-D agencies for payments to custodial families.

A New Partnership in Enforcement

The creation of a specialized collection agency at the federal level calls for a re-examination of the framework of federalism within which the child support system has been designed. In the traditional dual system of child support, both the enforcement of private support and the financing of public support are administered at the state level with joint funding from the federal and state governments. This division of labor cuts across all enforcement activities.

Yet federalization and centralization are advantageous if the tasks involved are of a routine nature: impersonal, mechanical, and without much need for discretionary decision-making. Martha Derthick found both SSA and IRS to be agencies under stress because of the voluminous set of regulations these agencies have to respond to, many of which are not well-defined and, as in disability review for eligibility, involve decisions on a case by case level.[27] But these agencies are efficient in carrying out the core function of routine tax collection and benefit payments.

Wage withholding fits the characterization of a routine task. Once the amount to be withheld has been determined, the implementation of the withholding order can be carried out according to a single set of procedures without significantly interfering with the local operation of the other elements of the child support system.

Since CSCD would be coordinated with the IRS or the SSA, current employment and earnings information would always be available at the agency's finger tips. This makes it possible for CSCD to revise awards efficiently. Each state would inform CSCD of the factors to be included in its formula for revising child support award. CSCD would compute the new amount of support obligation automatically for each case in need of review.

Under such a system, individual custodial or noncustodial families may be required to file with the agency updated information. For example, a custodial parent without tax liabilities in a particular year would nonetheless be required to file a tax form or risk losing the opportunity to have the support payment adjusted upward for the coming year.

Award adjustment through this automated process is of course not final. Both parents would have the opportunity to appeal. The appeal process would take place at the state level, with each state's own administrative or judicial processes. In the absence of protest, however, the adjusted amount would become the final award until the next review period.

In other words, CSCD plays the limited role of a processing agent, leaving discretionary decision-making in the hands of state-level IV-D agencies. With the federal agency taking up the "first cut" of the review process, the tasks of triennial review by state officials would likely be made considerably easier.

Limits of federalization

This proposal calls for the federalization of a limited enforcement function: the maintenance of a national registry of child support cases, the collection of child support through wage withholding and the preliminary periodic adjustment of award through automated processing. To the extent that other sources of income besides wages could be withheld on a routine basis as well, the collection of child support by withholding those incomes could also be part of the mandate of CSCD. For instance, if this federal collection agency is set up within the IRS, it would be relatively easy to intercept annual federal income tax refunds for all noncustodial parents with delinquent child support accounts.

Would more extensive versions of federalization be constructive? Federalizing award standard along with wage withholding has been proposed before.[28] The recent Downey-Hyde Child Support Enforcement and Assurance Proposal suggests an even greater role for the federal government.[29] It proposes essentially to eliminate the current system of federal-state partnership in child support enforcement. Under the Downey-Hyde proposal, after an initial amount of support award is officially established by a state or local agency according to a *federal* numeric standard, the federal government would take over all collection, adjustment of order, and parent location activities. Paternity determination would remain a function of the state at the state's option, but only if the state meets federally determined standards of performance.[30]

There are two major arguments against the federalization of all child support enforcement functions. First, many of these functions are intricately related to family and domestic relations, the regulation of which has always been the prerogatives of the states. It would be difficult for the system to operate under both federal and state regulations. For example, as long as family law remains within state jurisdiction, a uniform national standard, whether for initial award determination or revision, cannot operate without interfering with custody, visitation, remarriage, and a host of other legal issues.

The second problem is that of efficiency. Besides routine collections and preliminary revision of award, most other dimensions of child support enforcement do not have the features of routine processing. Therefore it is not clear how a federal enforcement apparatus could do any better than its state counterparts. Paternity determination is one such example. While parts of the process such as blood test are standardized, the identification and location of the noncustodial parents, as well as the personal rapport needed for soliciting the cooperation of the custodial parents, are highly personalized and labor-intensive. State and local authorities are more suitable for the task.

The argument can be made that the federal government would still be better equipped to deal with the interstate dimension of issues like paternity determination. However, if a routine parentage establishment process is available at the state level and if employment information is available at the federal level at CSCD, most of the complexity of pursuing interstate cases in the traditional system would be reduced to collection by withholding.

To retain the administration at the state level does not mean that the rules governing those tasks could not be standardized within a state. To improve state-level enforcement, each state should continue to institutionalize universal parental obligations through standardization of procedures. This is especially important with regards to parentage establishment, the least-developed dimension in the bureaucratization of enforcement. Specifically, individual states should

- Establish non-adversarial procedures for paternity acknowledgement. Hospital-based systems should be given top consideration;

- Require the recording of social security number on birth certificates although it is not mandated by federal legislation;

- Make parentage establishment mandatory for all infants. Educational campaigns and administrative measures should be carried out to solicit cooperation from custodial parents in the process of paternity determination. Guidelines for exemptions as well as for penalties for non-compliance should be set forth.

- Pass legislation to clarify visitation rights and to standardize penalties for violation. For example, Utah has passed law to allow for sentencing of custodial parents to community service if they violate visitation orders.

Other issues that require standardization at the state level include expedited procedures for applying numeric standards to set child support award, and the collaborative relationship between IV-A (welfare grants) and IV-D agencies in working with custodial parents on welfare.

The new model of federal collection would open up new ways of defining federal incentives. In the current system, federal incentive payments are based upon the amount of private child support collected by state IV-D agencies. With the takeover of the collection function by the federal government, incentive formulas for the states can now be redirected to other functions, foremost among which would be the pursuit of parentage identification. In this regard, the Downey-Hyde proposal represents a new approach. It proposes to provide federal matching funds specifically for paternity determination.[31]

Paternity determination later in the life of the child, especially in contested cases or in those involving the location of parents, shows the limitation of the bureaucratic enforcement of child support. Tracking down absent parents and bringing paternity suits require intensive resources, discretionary decisions, and individual attention that defies any standardization of procedures. Another child support enforcement function that cannot be bureaucratized is the collection of past due child support when the routinized collection mechanism fails to obtain full payments from the noncustodial parent.

These non-routine procedures must be delegated to some part of the bureaucratic network, but we will wait till chapter 7 to complete the design of this system.

Conclusion

While reforms up until the Family Support Act have created a federal-state system of administrative apparatus for child support enforcement, additional restructuring of this system is necessary to meet several pressing issues. These issues include: the need to establish parentage for every child, the need for review and adjustment of awards over time, and the need to collect support despite frequent job turnovers and interstate mobility of noncustodial parents. In addition, the enforcement bureaucracy needs to develop the capacity to collect arrearages as there will always be noncustodial parents delinquent on support obligations.

The proposal in this chapter deals with enforcement activities that can be routinized and standardized. It calls for the restructuring of the current network of enforcement so that the tax compliance model of child support responsibility can be more effectively applied. At the federal level, there ought to be a national child support registry linked up with federal tax records. A federal agency would be established to oversee this linked system. The mission of the agency is to (1) serve employers across the country with notices to withholding wages, (2) collect and disburse the withheld child support payments, and (3) provide preliminary revision of support award based on information in the tax records.

With the routine collection function transferred to the federal level, the state child support enforcement bureaucracies would concentrate on other elements of child support policy, including administrative procedures for universal establishment of parentage, expeditious determination of initial support award as well as future adjustment in the event the adjustment calculated by the federal agency is contested by either parent.

This new partnership between the federal and state bureaucracy assigns the automated activities to the federal level. This eliminates the institutional barriers between state agencies when the parents live in different states. The states, in turn, are responsible for tasks requiring flexibility and discretionary decision-making. The initial cost of setting up this federal-state enforcement system is likely to be expensive. Especially cumbersome would be the establishment of the national registry that interface with the information systems currently under development at individual states.[32] The long-term cost-effectiveness of such a system warrants the investment, however, since once the system is set up, the marginal cost of processing additional cases would be modest.

This proposal leaves unresolved the issue of how to carry out enforcement activities that cannot be standardized. This is an issue to be discussed in chapter 7 where we will put together a new model of child support system. Meanwhile, we will turn to the other two dimensions of child support policy, those that deal with the public's responsibilities in supporting children.

Notes for Chapter 4

1. National Commission on Children, *Beyond Rhetoric: A New American Agenda for Children and Families* (Washington DC: Government Printing Office, 1991), p.98.

2. U.S. House of Representatives, Committee on Ways and Means, *Child Support Enforcement Report Card* (Washington DC: Government Printing Office, 1991).

3. Martha Derthick, *Agency in Stress: The Social Security Administration in American Government* (Washington, DC: Brookings Institution 1990) especially pp. 82-87.

4. Census Bureau's surveys of the child support population include custodial mothers only.

5. Andrea H. Beller and John W. Graham, "Child Support Payments :Evidence from Repeated Cross Sections" *American Economic Review*, (1988): 81-85.

6. The proposals for change in the private child support system in this chapter focus on small-scale innovative approaches. The information on the various programs adopted or proposals by different states cited therein is obtained through interviews conducted with various state child support enforcement agencies.

7. Ann Nichols-Casebolt and Irwin Garfinkel, "Trends in Paternity Adjudication and Child Support Awards," *Social Science Quarterly* 72 (1991): 83-97.

8. U.S. House of Representatives, Committee on Ways and Means, *Overview of Entitlement Programs: 1992 Green Book* (Washington, DC: Government Printing Office, 1992).

9. The probability of a marriage to avert nonmarital birth has also gone down over the years, from 52 percent in the early 1960s to 27 percent in the late 1980s. See U.S. Bureau of the Census, Current Population Reports, Series P-20, No. 454, *Fertility of American Women: June 1990* (Washington, DC: Government Printing Office, 1991).

10. Laboratory tests for paternity determination are excluded from the computation of administrative cost.

11. U.S. Department of Health and Human Service, Office of Child Support Enforcement, *Twelfth Annual Report to Congress* (Washington, DC: OCSE, 1987), Table 25.

12. U.S. Bureau of the Census, Current Population Reports, Series P-60, No. 173, *Child Support and Alimony: 1989* (Washington, DC: U.S. Government Printing Office, 1991).

13. Esther Wattenberg, "Establishment of Paternity for Nonmarital Children: Do Policy and Practice Discourage Adjudication?" *Public Welfare* 45 (1987:3): 8-13.

14. U.S. General Accounting Office, *Child Support: Need to Improve Efforts to Identify Fathers and Obtain Support Orders*. GAO/HRD-87-37 (Washington, DC: GAO, April 1987).

15. U.S. Commission on Interstate Child Support, *Supporting Our Children: A Blueprint for Reform*. A Report to Congress, August 1992, p. 7-11.

16. Charles F. Adams, Jr., David Landsbergen, and Larry Cobler, "Welfare Reform and Paternity Establishment: A Social Experiment," *Journal of Policy Analysis and Management* 11 (1992): 665-687.

17. Esther Wattenberg, "Establishment of Paternity for Nonmarital Children: Do Policy and Practice Discourage Adjudication?" p. 12.

18. *Ibid.*

19. Ann Nichols-Casebolt, Irwin Garfinkel, and Pat Wong, "Reforming Wisconsin's Child Support System," in Sheldon Danziger and John F. Witte, eds., *State Policy Choices: The Wisconsin Experience* (Madison, WI: University of Wisconsin Press (1988).

20. Irwin Garfinkel, Donald Oellerich, and Philip K. Robins, "Child Support Guidelines: Will They Make a Difference?" *Journal of Family Issues* 12 (1991): 404-429.

21. "Review and Adjustment: Early Results," *Child Support Report* 13 (1991:5) p.4.

22. Ann R. Gordon et al., *Income Withholding, Medical Support, and Services to Non-AFDC Cases After the Child Support Amendments of 1984.* Report to U.S. Department of Health and Human Services, May 1991.

23. Carol Welch,"Employer Reporting Program: Longitudinal Report: July 1990- January 1992," Washington State Office of Support Enforcement, Washington State Department of Social and Health Services, July 1992.

24. U.S. General Accounting Office, *Interstate Child Support: Wage Withholding not Fulfilling Expectations.* GA)/HRD-92-65BR (Washington, DC: GAO, February 1992), pp. 42-46.

25. Roy L. Weaver and Robert G. Williams, "Problems with URESA: Interstate Child Support Enforcement Isn't Working But Could" (Paper presented at the Third National Child Support Conference, American Bar Association, Washington, DC, 1989).

26. U.S. Commission on Interstate Child Support, *Supporting Our Children*, p. 13-5.

27. Martha Derthick, *Agency under Stress*, pp. 205-209.

28. Archibald Stuart, "Rescuing Children: Reforms in the Child Support Payment System," *Social Service Review* 60 (1986): 201-217.

29. "The Downey/Hyde Child Support Enforcement and Assurance Proposal: Promoting Parental Responsibility and Securing a Better Future for Children in America." Background paper released by Representative Downey's office, May 12, 1992.

30. "The Downey/Hyde Child Support Enforcement And Assurance Proposal," various papers released May 12, 1992.

31. "The Downey/Hyde Child Support Enforcement and Assurance Proposal," p.2.

32. Testimony by Michael R. Henry before the Subcommittee on Human Resources, Committee on Ways and Means, U.S. House of Representatives, July 1, 1992.

5

Reformulating Public Child Support

Focusing reform measures on private child support has its obvious appeals. From a fiscal standpoint, the private child support system does not expend tax dollars as benefit payments. Perhaps more important is its moral message. In an era of conservatism, reforms in private child support unambiguously identify absent fathers as villains; and the cost of enforcing child support payment is relatively easy to justify as holding noncustodial parents accountable for the obligation to their children.

It is therefore no surprise that welfare reform for the last fifteen years has promulgated increasingly stringent measures to address the enforcement elements of child support policy: parentage establishment, award determination, and support collection.

If the objectives of child support policy are limited to enforcing noncustodial parent obligations, these measures alone are sufficient. If the objectives also include the enhancement of the economic well-being and self-sufficiency of custodial families, however, enforcement measures alone are hardly adequate. Research by Oellerich, Garfinkel, and Robins indicates that even if the private support system expands to its full potential--establishing an award for *every* custodial family and successfully collecting from *all* noncustodial parents under widely adopted child support guidelines-- welfare caseload nationwide would go down by only 16 percent and poverty gap would be reduced by 30 percent.[1]

Yet it is highly unlikely that the private enforcement system can operate anywhere near full efficiency. Furthermore, to the extent that low-income custodial parents are more likely to be victims of imperfect enforcement, the actual impact of private child support reform on the economic status of custodial families is even weaker. Something in addition to the private child support system needs to be in place for the economic protection of the children in these families.

Through the Family Support Act, Congress has at least implicitly acknowledged the need to provide the support structure for work so that custodial parents can be financially independent. Yet the issue of public financial protection for children in single-parent families has remained stagnant throughout the history of welfare reform. The notion of public child support benefit as a minimum guarantee to *replace* earnings has remained intact. Work expense deductions may have been more or less generous at different points, and work expectation may have become more explicit over time, but the work-discouraging nature of the AFDC program has not changed.

In the next step to reform the public child support system, the objective should be to design a program of financial protection that *supplements* earnings.

The Concept of Child Support Assurance

Child support assurance is a proposal to implement this objective. The idea of child support assurance has its origin in Scandinavian countries[2] where it is known as advance maintenance. In its generic form, advance maintenance provides each custodial family with a public amount of child support, depending only on the number of eligible children in the family. The amount is paid on a regular basis, ahead of the actual payment by the noncustodial parent and unaffected by the economic status of the custodial family.

The private support subsequently collected is used to reimburse the advance maintenance account. If private support payment exceeds advance maintenance, the custodial family receives the difference and no public expenditures are incurred. In this case the public program amounts to a very short-term, interest-free loan to the custodial family.

If private support payment falls below the advanced amount, however, the custodial family is allowed to keep the maintenance payment. The amount in excess of private payment would be the public supplement for this family. Irwin Garfinkel is the leading advocate of this concept in the country. He has dubbed it child support assurance because it essentially assures a minimum level of child support for each custodial family.[3]

A public child support system with a child support assurance would, at least initially, co-exist with the current welfare program. As a program with broader eligibility, the assurance benefit would have to be lower than AFDC benefit to keep government costs neutral. A custodial parent with no income besides the assurance payment would still be eligible for AFDC. The assurance benefit in this case would be treated as unearned income. In other words, a family participating in both programs would receive the same amount of public child support as before, without any change in public expenditures.

What the assurance program would likely do, however, is to make employment more rewarding for custodial parents and therefore reduce dependency on welfare. To see how this might be the case, we will consider a hypothetical custodial mother with two children, and we will explore the options available to this family in terms of work hours and program participation, under the current system and under a system that includes a child support assurance benefit.

A hypothetical family

This family consists of a custodial mother and two children. They have no unearned sources of income, not even private child support. There are three scenarios to consider. In each scenario we will assume that the mother is free to decide on her level of work efforts, measured by the number of hours worked, including the choice of not working at all.

In the first scenario, the mother relies on employment as her sole source of income. This scenario represents a non-AFDC custodial mother.

The current public child support system is represented in the second scenario. We will use the AFDC guarantee for a family of three in the median state[4] in 1992, or $372, as her monthly AFDC benefits if she does not work. To simplify, we will also assume that, after the allowed deductions, AFDC benefits will decrease by two-thirds of the amount of her earnings. That is, for every dollar she earns, her total income increases by just 33 cents.

In the third scenario, the family is under a reformed public child support system consisting of a child support assurance. The assurance benefit is available regardless of the amount of earnings by the custodial mother. This scenario represents the complete replacement of the current AFDC program by the assurance program. For now we will set the assurance amount at 60 percent of the AFDC guarantee, or $223 per month.[5]

Suppose this mother commands the minimum wage when she joins the labor market. For ease of exposition, her net wage would be $4 per hour after deduction for social security. It is now a simple matter to represent her total income as a function of the number of hours worked in each scenario.

In Scenario (1), her income (Y) per month is equivalent to her earnings, represented as wage multiplied by hours (H) of work:

$$(1) \qquad Y = 4H$$

A full-time work schedule of 160 hours would result in total monthly income of $640.

In Scenario (2), she receives the AFDC guarantee of $372 per month if she does not work. As her work hours increase, however, she essentially gets to keep only one-third of her earnings since the rest would be offset by a reduction in her AFDC benefits. Therefore:

$$(2) \qquad Y = (372 - 2.67\,H) + 4\,H$$
$$= 372 + 1.32\,H$$

Equation (2) represents the relationship between total income and the number of work hours while she is on AFDC as long as the amount $372\text{-}2.67H$ is greater than zero. When the number of hours worked is high enough to reduce $372\text{-}2.67H$ to zero, the family will no longer be eligibility for AFDC and Scenario (2) will not be available.

In Scenario (3), there is no reduction in child support assurance as earnings increase, so

$$(3) \qquad Y = 223 + 4\,H$$

Each of these equations is a budget line representing how the family's purchasing power changes as the mother's work effort changes in each of the policy scenario. In reality, these are not isolated scenarios. Rather, they are co-existing options from which a custodial parent could choose. The question is: how many hours would a custodial mother have to work to be ineligible for AFDC under a system without child support assurance, and how many hours would she have to work to be off AFDC when an assurance benefit is available?

By design, AFDC eligibility expires when a non-AFDC alternative results in the same total family income as the AFDC alternative. This means that a family becomes ineligible for AFDC at the number of work hours for which the resulting income in scenario (2) is equal to the income for the same work effort in either of the other scenarios, or equivalently, when the budget lines are equal between the AFDC scenario and a non-AFDC scenario.

When the only alternative to AFDC is scenario (1), the hypothetical family becomes ineligible for AFDC at H=139 hours per month, with a resulting income of $556. On the other hand, when one compares scenarios (2) and (3), AFDC eligibility runs out as soon as H reaches 56 hours, at which point the monthly family income is $447. Under scenario (3), if the mother continues to work through 139 hours, her total monthly income becomes $779, considerably higher than in Scenario (1).

The presence of child support assurance, as illustrated in this example, makes it easier for custodial parents to work their way out of the current welfare system. Without any guaranteed child support, the parent in our hypothetical example has to work almost full time in order to achieve an income comparable to the AFDC benefits. Under a system with a child support assurance, she only needs to work somewhat over one-quarter time to earn an amount comparable to welfare. That is the advantage of child support assurance over AFDC. Since its receipt is not affected by earnings, there are more incentives for a custodial family to gain financial independence.

The universal nature of child support assurance leads to the obvious problem of cost containment. Since in its generic form the assurance program provides an income floor to all custodial families, it is bound to be expensive for the public treasury. Without some sort of cost control features accompanying the program, we would simply spend in the form of assurance payments what we save in welfare reduction, and perhaps much more.

The fact that our hypothetical custodial family receives no private support payment accentuates this problem. The more private support is paid by the noncustodial parent, the less the government has to supplement the custodial family in the form of assurance payment. Other cost control measures may include limiting eligibility to subgroups of custodial families, or phasing out the assurance payment on the basis of custodial family income. We will return to this issue as we examine specific proposals in the next section.

Administration

Welfare reduction is not the only purpose of child support assurance. Assurance benefit is also a mechanism to eliminate the insecurity of fluctuations in child support payments by noncustodial parents. To support this assertion and consider any potential difficulties in its implementation, we briefly consider the administration of a child support assurance program below.

The existing welfare bureaucracy in each state is already sending out AFDC checks to low-income custodial families once a month. With the introduction of an assurance program, a check will be sent each month to all custodial parents regardless of income.

For the first month a custodial family enters the child support system, the amount of the check would be equal to the assurance level plus, if applicable, the amount of AFDC benefits for which the family is still eligible based on the record of her own resource level. The government meanwhile collects that family's private child support for that month from the noncustodial parent. Any amount of private child support in excess of the assurance level will be credited to the custodial family's account for a larger check the following month. If, on the other hand, the private payment is less than the assurance level, the check for the following month will again be at the level of the assurance benefit. This cycle of collection and disbursement will repeat itself, with the use of an automated information system.

Thus the administrative burdens incurred by a child support assurance program are, first, the increased number of checks, compared to the AFDC program, that have to be sent each month since all custodial families in the child support system are involved. In this regard, it should be noted that state IV-D programs are already taking part in collection and disbursement for some non-AFDC custodial families, so the increase in the number of checks owing to the assurance program should not be inordinate. Second, there will be a time lag of one month between disbursement of assurance benefits and the collection of private support payment. The increase in steadiness of payment under the assurance system would seem to make this tradeoff worthwhile.

To summarize, if the concept of an assurance benefit is incorporated in its generic form, the U.S. child support system would be changed in two fundamental ways. First, since the assurance payment is not a function of a custodial parent's income, it would not be reduced as the earnings of the custodial parent increase. The disincentive to work embedded in the traditional American public child support program of AFDC will thus be eliminated.

Second, child support assurance would better integrate the nation's child support policy. Since the assurance program covers all custodial families regardless of economic background, the distinction between the current public and private systems as well as the stigma attached to the public child support system would be minimized.

This is how child support assurance would operate in theory. In practice, there are many policy questions that have to be resolved. Foremost among them is the question of government cost containment. Below is a discussion of two programs proposed at the state level and the way they have addressed the issue of cost containment.

The Wisconsin Proposal

The Wisconsin Child Support Assurance System (CSAS) was proposed in the early 1980s as a joint effort between researchers headed by Irwin Garfinkel at the Institute for Research on Poverty, and the State of Wisconsin.[6] CSAS was proposed as a comprehensive plan to reform the child support system. It includes a number of changes in the enforcement of private support along with the child support assurance benefit. Many of the changes actually dated before the 1984 and 1988 federal welfare reforms, putting Wisconsin ahead of the country in standardizing the enforcement of private support.

Specifically, a presumptive percentage-of-income standard for setting child support award was implemented in 1983, a year before the passage of the federal legislation that required numeric standards as guidelines. The Wisconsin standard sets child support at 17% of noncustodial parent's gross income for one child, and 25%, 29%, 31% and 34% for 2 to 5 or more children respectively. CSAS also requires immediate income withholding for all noncustodial parents as of 1987.

The child support assurance (CSA) component of the Wisconsin plan is the first such proposal in the United States. It was never implemented, however, largely owing to political events within the state government.[7] Nonetheless it serves as an important model for the present discussion on the public child support system.

The original Wisconsin proposal defines as eligible for child support assurance all custodial families *who have received a formal award* of private child support, regardless of their income level or AFDC recipiency. The advantage of requiring support award for CSA eligibility is its incentive for custodial parents to cooperate with the government, if necessary, to identify the noncustodial parent and to establish a formal child support award. Since a formal award is a pre-requisite to efficient collection, this requirement also makes private support payment more probable. However, by not making income an eligibility criterion, the program is at risk of incurring runaway expenditures if a sizable group of noncustodial parents do not pay an amount above the level of publicly assured benefits.

In order to control cost and to avoid adverse redistribution (when, for example, the assured benefits are given to an occasional wealthy custodial family with an unemployed noncustodial parent), the CSAS proposal includes a surtax on the custodial family's incomes other than child support.

A plausible method defining the rate of the custodial parent surtax is the use of the same percentage-of-income standard that determines the support obligation of the noncustodial parent. This surtax symbolizes the equivalent responsibility expected of the custodial parent to provide for the children. If the custodial surtax is the same as the absent parent child support standard, then a custodial family receiving the child support assurance would be taxed at 17 percent if there is one child in the family, and 25 percent if there are two, and so on. The surtax would cease to operate when the original amount of assurance benefit has been completely recovered by the government.

Graphic Analysis

Figure 5.1 illustrates how the CSA program supplements the existing public child support system. This figure represents the situation of most concern in public policy: private child support payment (TC) falls significantly below the AFDC guarantee (TA).

If a custodial family is not enrolled in AFDC, its income would increase along the line segment CD as the custodial parent works more hours. If a custodial family receives AFDC benefits, its income rises much more slowly, along segment AF, due to the offset of AFDC benefits. These two budget segments represent scenarios (1) and (2) in our hypothetical example. It should also be noted that the vertical distance between the two budget lines AF and CD represents the amount of government payment, through AFDC in this case, at each given level of work effort.

Now an assurance benefit (TB) is set at a level below TA.[8] As shown in the figure, TB exceeds TC. If TB were below TC, that is, if the noncustodial parent had paid more than the assurance level, the income of the family would be the same with or without the assurance benefits

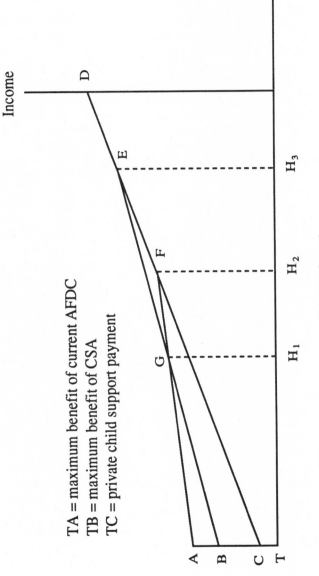

Figure 5.1
Wisconsin Child Support Assurance (CSA)

TA = maximum benefit of current AFDC
TB = maximum benefit of CSA
TC = private child support payment

Income

Hours of work

because the government would be reimbursed the entire amount of the assurance benefits.

Given an assurance level that is greater than the private child support received, TB represents the basic income for a custodial family if the custodial parent does not work. If this family is also enrolled in AFDC, its basic income jumps to TA and the assurance program becomes irrelevant to her because she would still face the budget line AF as before. However, if she does not participate in AFDC, her option would be represented by BE as she begins to work. Again the vertical distance of the budget options BE above the budget options CD measures the amount of government supplement for each level of work hours, this time through the CSA program.

Without the custodial parent surtax, both budget lines BE and CD would have the same slope, representing the market wage rate of the custodial parent. This would lead to an enormous amount of subsidy, however, as the supplement would remain constant even for custodial families with a lot of earnings. The custodial surtax in the Wisconsin proposal would reduce the effective wage rate of the custodial parent, but by a much smaller amount than the AFDC benefit reduction rate. Therefore the budget line BE in Figure 5.1 has a flatter slope than the non-CSA budget line of CD. At point E the two lines converge, indicating the complete recovery of the initial public supplement of child support. From that point on the surtax disappears.

The figure also confirms the idea that child support assurance makes it easier to "work off" AFDC, since the number of hours H_1 required to exceed AFDC eligibility when the assurance benefit is available, is less onerous than H_2, the level of work needed in the absence of assurance. This intuitive notion has a counterpart in the economic theory of labor supply.

Labor supply behavior

Economic theory suggests that, everything else being equal, an increase in unearned income would discourage work effort. This is the expected impact of an assurance program on non-AFDC custodial parent whose private support, originally at TC, would now be raised to the higher level, TB, of the assurance benefit. Thus the CSAS program is expected to reduce the work effort of custodial parents who are not AFDC recipients.

For custodial parents receiving welfare, however, the availability of the assurance benefit does not have the effect of an increased unearned income, because the assurance level is lower than the original AFDC guarantee. Rather, the effect of the assurance program is to enhance employment and self-sufficiency as an alternative to welfare by making a higher effective wage rate attainable, as represented by the difference in slope between the AFDC budget line AF and the CSA budget line BE in the figure.

Theoretically, an increase in wage rate has two opposing effects. Through what is known as the wage effect, labor supply is predicted to increase because the reward of work is now higher. A wage increase also has an income effect, however. As the total earnings of the custodial parent increase because of the higher wage rate, she can afford to cut back on her hours and still stay at the same income level as before. The net effect of a wage increase would theoretically be the balance of these two effects.

As an empirical issue, however, for low-income female heads of households, the wage effect in general outweighs the income effect.[9] Employment, made more attractive by the income floor TB through the assurance program, is therefore expected to increase and consequently induce some custodial parents to choose the budget segment BE instead of the AFDC budget line of AF. That is, some of the custodial parents on welfare would work for self-sufficiency under the new program.

As these custodial parents leave AFDC, government expenditures on that program will decrease. In addition, the CSAS reform measures in enforcement are also expected to increase private child support collection, again reimbursing the government for some of the current welfare expenditures. These savings will in turn offset the costs of the new CSA program. In practice, the feasibility of CSAS depends on the answers to some central policy questions, such as the cost of the new program relative to current AFDC expenditures, and the magnitude of welfare caseload reduction resulting from increased private collections and from the economic incentives created by the assurance benefit.

Impact of CSAS in Wisconsin

While empirical answers to these questions would only be available after the CSAS proposal has been implemented, these questions can be assessed, on the basis of the above theoretical prediction as well as empirical evidence about the size of these effects, through micro-simulation modeling.

The structure of the new program can be incorporated into a simulation model and its impacts evaluated if a data set of custodial parents is available that contains information on current labor supply behavior, income, and program participation status. This simulation model would predict the impact of the CSAS proposal on custodial parent labor supply and program participation decision. Since labor supply determines earnings under the child support assurance program, family income, poverty status, and government expenditures can also be predicted from the model. In addition, changes in the performance of private child support enforcement mechanisms also have to be simulated if the changes are not already reflected in the data set.

A simulation model has been used to assess the effects of the CSA reform in the State of Wisconsin itself.

The methodology used in the modeling process is described in the Appendix.[10] This section will describe the results of the simulation research.[11]

The data set consists of a sample of 4,977 custodial families in Wisconsin in 1985.[12] That year, 46 percent of all Wisconsin custodial families participated in AFDC, which had an annual expenditure of $373 million in benefit payments to custodial families. These custodial families had very low levels of work effort, at an average of 105 hours per year. Custodial parents not on welfare, on the other hand, had substantial employment activities. The average labor supply for that group was 1,418 hours in that year.

The data set also indicates that aggregate private child support payments among all custodial families amounted to $134 million. About 54 percent of the families had an award. The data represents the status of the child support system before any element of the CSAS was in place.

The results of the simulation are summarized in Table 5.1. The top three rows predict the impact of the improvements in *private* child support enforcement only, without the introduction of any assurance benefit. If all cases in the system are subject to the Wisconsin percentage-of-income standard in setting award but there is no change in the number of families with an award or in the efficiency of collection, the expected impacts are minimal: the government would collect an additional $4 million to offset current AFDC outlays; and the reduction in welfare and poverty would be 2 percent and 8 percent respectively.

However, the award establishment and collection levels are expected to improve. More custodial families would obtain awards to be eligible for the assurance benefits. The percentage of private support debts actually collected would rise in the long run as the system of immediate wage withholding continues. The impacts with the improvement in these two dimensions in the enforcement system are described in the next two rows, where award rate and collection rate each rises to a level expect-

Table 5.1

Estimated Effects of CSAS in Wisconsin
by Program Components, 1985[a]

Component[b]	Net Savings[c] ($ Millions)	% Reduction in AFDC Caseload	% Reduction in Poverty Gap	% Change in Hours of Work AFDC Families	Non-AFDC Families	All Families
Uniform percentage standard only	$ 4	2%	8%	+8%	-2%	-2%
Medium improvement in awards	13	2%	14%	+11%	-3%	-2%
Medium improvement in collections	24	3%	16%	+14%	-3%	-2%
Child support assurance ($3,000)	20	3%	16%	+16%	-4%	-1%

[a] Percentages are calculated using averages before CSAS. Net savings are in millions of 1985 dollars.
[b] Components are added cummulatively.
[c] Savings are based on changes in AFDC and CSA expenditures, as well as changes in income tax revenues resulting from differences in earnings, before and after the CSAS system is in place.

Source: Irwin Garfinkel, Philip K. Robins, Pat Wong, and Daniel R. Meyer, "The Wisconsin Child Support Assurance System: Estimated Effects on Poverty, Labor Supply, Caseload, and Costs," p.22.

ed to be reasonably attainable for the system, labelled here as "medium" improvement.[13] Government savings increase three-folds with the improvement in award establishment, and double again to $24 million a year when the level of collections also improve.

These savings are the result of custodial parents leaving AFDC. Part of the reason for the decrease in AFDC enrollment is ineligibility resulted from the increased child support payments. Other parents leave welfare because the private support collected makes working for self-sufficiency possible, as indicated by the small but gradual increase in labor supply among the original AFDC recipients. Also consistent with economic theory, the non-AFDC custodial parents show slight declines in work effort as their unearned incomes increase because of the rise in private collections.

The estimated impacts of the *assurance benefits* are presented in the last row, assuming that the previous improvements in the private system are cumulative. That is, if on top of the changes in the private system we also implement the CSA program, savings would drop from $24 million to $20 million. The reductions in welfare caseload and in poverty, however, remain unchanged, at 3 percent and 16 percent respectively.

The decrease in savings should be of no surprise since CSA is a spending program. What is important is the small magnitude of the decrease. As private child support collections increase to the medium level of improvement, many noncustodial parents would be paying an amount of private child support above the assurance level. Therefore there would be little difference, in terms of welfare and poverty reductions, between this scenario and the one with private support improvement but without the assurance benefit.

As long as the enforcement of private child support improves to the level expected in the simulation, an assurance benefit of $3,000 in Wisconsin is insignificant relative to the child support payments, public or private, of the majority of the custodial parents in that state. The assurance benefit is still important, however, as a buffer against irregularities in payments.

Thus the Wisconsin results indicate that, at an assurance level of $3,000 for one child, the CSAS would not be costly. It would actually save the public a small amount of money, about 5 percent relative to the AFDC expenditures of $373 million in that state. The effects on AFDC reduction that could be attributed to the assurance program would also be insignificant, however. The lack of AFDC reduction effect is due to the high AFDC benefit level in Wisconsin. At about $5,500 per year for a custodial family with one child, it is almost twice the amount of the assurance benefit of $3,000.

In order for the assurance program to be competitive with the AFDC program, therefore, the assurance level would have to be set at very high level in high-benefit states like Wisconsin. Since most other states have much lower AFDC benefit guarantee, a nationwide child support assurance program may have more of an impact even at a lower assurance level.

Impact of CSAS Nationwide

This expectation of larger nationwide impacts is borne out by simulation research by Meyer, Garfinkel, Oellerich, and Robins.[14] Their research simulates the impacts of the Wisconsin CSAS proposal implemented nationwide with uniform assurance benefits. The only major difference in the nationwide plan is that, instead of a special custodial parent tax, the public supplement portion of the assurance benefit is subject to the federal income tax. Applying the same simulation model used in the Wisconsin study to a national data set of child-support-eligible mothers, collected by the Census Bureau[15], these researchers have reported the results shown in Table 5.2.

The top half of the table shows the impacts of child support assurance, implemented nationwide at various level of benefits, without concomitant improvements in

Table 5.2

Estimated Effects of CSA in the United States, by Levels of Assurance Benefit[a]

Scenario[b]	Net Savings[a] ($ Millions)	% Reduction in AFDC Caseload	% Reduction in Poverty Gap	% Change in Hours of Work		
				AFDC Families	Non-AFDC Families	All Families
Child support system as in U.S., 1985						
CSA = $0	$0	0%	0%	0%	0%	0%
CSA = $1,000	- 448	3%	2%	5%	0%	0%
CSA = $2,000	- 1,759	8%	5%	15%	-1%	1%
CSA = $3,000	- 4,239	13%	9%	26%	-1%	1%
Child support system with medium improvement in awards and collections						
CSA = $0	1,026	8%	10%	9%	-3%	-2%
CSA = $1,000	943	11%	12%	13%	-3%	-1%
CSA = $2,000	461	18%	15%	24%	-3%	0%
CSA = $3,000	- 850	28%	21%	45%	-3%	1%

[a] Savings are based on changes in AFDC and CSA expenditures, as well as changes in income tax revenues resulting from differences in earnings, before and after the CSAS system is in place.

Source: Daniel R. Meyer, Irwin Garfinkel, Donald T. Oellerich, and Philip K. Robins, "Who Should Be Eligible for an Assured Child Support Benefit?" p.174, based on 1986 Current Population Survey data.

the private child support system. Assuming each custodial mother to have received the exact amount of private support as reported in the 1985 Census Bureau survey, an assurance level of $3,000 would reduce AFDC caseload in that year by 13 percent. This leads to a 26 percent rise in work effort by this group of custodial parents who no longer face the high benefit reduction rate AFDC imposes. Without any improvements in private support, however, the new system is expected to cost $4.2 billion a year.

Lower assurance level would result in less reduction in poverty and in welfare caseload. The largest proportionate changes are found in the net cost of the program. With the private child support system fixed at its 1985 level, an increase of assured benefit from $2,000 to $3,000 would raise the cost of the system by one-and-a-half time, from 1.76 to 4.24 billion dollars.

When medium level of improvements in the private child support system is included, private support collection would increase by slightly more than $1 billion, as shown in the first row of the bottom half of the table. The additional child support collections are expected to drive costs down significantly. In fact, up to an assurance level of $2,000, the new program is expected to save money relative to the current AFDC-only system.

The reduction in AFDC caseload when medium improvements are taken into account is due to the larger number of families eligible for assurance benefit when more awards are established. Taken together, the improved performance of the private child support system along with an assurance benefit of $2,000 would reduce poverty by 15 percent and AFDC caseload by 18 percent. If the assurance benefit is increased to $3,000 instead, more than a quarter of the nation's AFDC caseload would disappear, a considerably larger impact than that shown in Wisconsin alone. The cost of the program would remain small, however. In fact, as long as the assurance level is not much beyond $2,000, the new program is predicted to cost less than the current AFDC system.

The child support assurance proposed in the Wisconsin CSAS plan is one of the approaches of changing the incentive structure of the AFDC system. While the Wisconsin version makes the assurance available without regard to income, the State of New York has adopted the idea of child support assurance *into* its welfare system. By restricting eligibility to custodial families on welfare, the New York plan lacks the universal, preventive nature of the Wisconsin proposal, but it has its advantage in containing the cost of such a program.

The New York Child Assistance Program

While the assured benefit component of the Wisconsin proposal lingered in state politics, the idea was being considered by New York. In a well known report to Governor Mario Cuomo at the end of 1986, New York's Task Force on Poverty and Welfare recommended the adoption of a child support assurance as one of many strategies in "rethinking the nature and purpose of public assistance."[16] Finally, New York opted to implement on an experimental basis a version of assurance benefit called Child Assistance Program (CAP).

CAP is different from the Wisconsin version in its approach to cost containment. Eligibility for CAP is restricted to AFDC custodial families with an award for private support.

In terms of its impetus to encourage and support the employment of custodial parents, CAP is designed to be more aggressive. Since the Wisconsin version covers welfare and non-welfare custodial families alike, it has to resort to a tax-back mechanism to phase out benefits for those with significant earnings. CAP controls cost by restricting eligibility, so it has less need for a high surtax. In the version implemented in several experimental counties,[17] CAP sets the basic benefit--its equivalent of child support assurance--at two-thirds of the AFDC guarantee. The earnings of a custodial parent only reduce

Figure 5.2
New York Child Assistance Program (CAP)

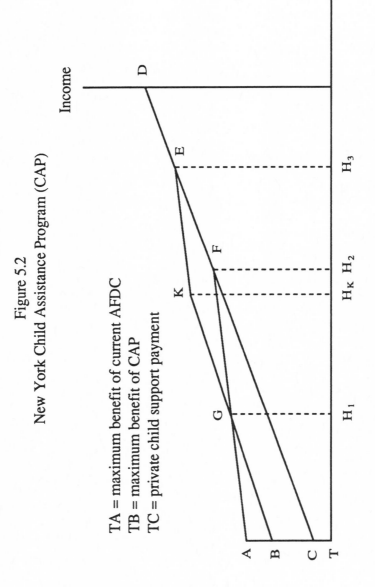

TA = maximum benefit of current AFDC
TB = maximum benefit of CAP
TC = private child support payment

her CAP benefits by ten cents for each dollar earned, until her earnings reach the poverty level, at which point the reduction rate of the regular AFDC program becomes effective. (See Figure 5.2).

This benefit structure keeps the effective tax rate on work relatively low for custodial families in poverty. It also allows a family to remain a CAP recipient even after family income exceeds the federal poverty line. In contrast, a family of three under the existing AFDC program in New York would have its welfare benefits completely phased out before reaching three-quarters of the poverty level.[18]

In addition to benefit structure, the CAP program has additional features aimed at increasing custodial family income and encouraging work. Food stamp benefits and child care allowance are both provided in cash. Case management services are specially organized for experimental CAP participants to facilitate employment activities. Unlike traditional AFDC but similar to the Wisconsin proposal, there is no limit on family savings or assets for CAP eligibility. Finally, in an effort to emphasize the distraction between CAP and welfare, field offices for the CAP program are separate from regular public assistance offices.

The long-term impact of the CAP program will not be known for some time, but an interim evaluation of the first 12 months of CAP arrived at the following conclusions.[19] Custodial parents participating in CAP worked more than those in the control group who received regular AFDC in the same counties. CAP parents who worked had 25 percent more earnings than parents in the control group.

While there was no significant difference between the experimental and control groups in private support collections, custodial parents in the experimental group who had the CAP option but who did not have a support order at the beginning were 50 percent more likely to have obtained a formal child support order by the end of the year. This is consistent with the expectation that assurance benefits provide incentives for custodial parents to establish an award. The interim evaluation also showed that there exists no significant difference in government benefit expenditures--counting both AFDC and CAP--between the experimental and the control groups.

Comparison of Alternatives

The Wisconsin CSA program and the New York CAP program represent two ways of restructuring the existing public child support system of AFDC. Both programs require the official establishment of private support award as a condition for participation. Both rely on the principle of low benefit reduction rate (relative to AFDC) for work incentive. The major difference is that the Wisconsin proposal would be universal among all custodial families with a private support order, while the New York proposal would restrict eligibility to those currently on welfare.

We have earlier alluded to the worry that, without any cost containment measure, an assurance program would provide significant amount of benefits to custodial families with high earnings. Both the Wisconsin and the New York programs provide cost containment measures. The former controls expenditures by levying a custodial parent surtax, and the latter primarily by restricting eligibility.

Table 5.3 presents how family income and government expenditures on our earlier hypothetical family with no private child support change under the current AFDC system, CSA, and CAP. The assumptions in the discussion of the hypothetical family still hold: the AFDC system has a guarantee of $372 per month, and the CSA and CAP guarantees are set at 60 percent of the AFDC guarantee, or at $223 per month.[20] The custodial parent has a net wage of $4 in the top half of the table. While a family on AFDC starts with higher level of benefit income, its total income increases more slowly as hours of work increase. When the

Table 5.3

Comparison of Three Public Child Support Plans, for Hypothetical Family of Three Receiving No Child Support

	AFDC Current System	CSA Wisconsin version	CAP New York version
Private payment	$ 0	$ 0	$ 0
Public guarantee[a]	$372	$223	$223
Custodial tax rate	0.67	0.25	0.10 [b]

Net wage = $4

Hours	Net earnings	Family income	Gov't cost	Family income	Gov't cost	Family income	Gov't cost
0	$ 0	$372	$372	$223	$223	$223	$223
40	160	425	265	343	183	367	207
80	320	478	159	463	143	511	191
120	480	532	52	583	103	655	175
160	640	640	0	703	63	799	159

Net wage = $6

Hours	Net earnings	Family income	Gov't cost	Family income	Gov't cost	Family income	Gov't cost
0	$ 0	$372	$372	$223	$223	$223	$223
40	240	452	212	403	163	493	199
80	480	532	52	583	103	655	175
120	720	720	0	763	4	871	151
160	960	640	0	1,063	0	1,056 [b]	96 [b]

[a] AFDC guarantee is set at the median among all states for 1992. CSA and CAP guarantees are set at 60% of AFDC guarantee.

[b] Custodial tax rate in CAP is set at 10% for earnings below poverty, and 67% for earnings above. The higher rate is effective only in the last row of the New York column, and only to the last $55 of earnings, since the poverty line for this family in 1992 is $905 per month.

custodial parent is working up to half-time, she would be better off enrolling in either of the new programs instead of AFDC.

In terms of how government costs are reduced as the mother works more hours, the New York program by design extends government support to high level of earnings because of its low benefit reduction rate. This is justified as lifting welfare families out of poverty, but it also keeps families on welfare longer.

As the wage rate of the custodial parent increases from $4 to $6 per hour, the burden on the public treasury declines. This decline is not nearly as dramatic as the decline resulting from private child support payment, however. Table 5.4 shows the income and government cost on the same hypothetical family, except that now the family receives $160 per month in private child support, the average amount received by custodial families in poverty. As the table illustrates, this level of private child support results in no net expenditures in the CSA program by the time the custodial parent works more than one-quarter time. Private child support also brings down the expenditures in the New York program on the hypothetical family considerably. These results confirm the importance of private child support collection in the financing of assurance programs. In fact, fiscally responsible assurance programs must be predicated upon an efficient mechanism of collecting private payment.

At that level of work efforts the family would still be better off staying on AFDC, however, since the AFDC alternative provides a much higher base amount due to the $50 private support set-aside. Because of this, the AFDC program would provide a higher amount of total income than CSA does, until the family's eligibility runs out, for both the lower-wage and higher-wage scenarios.

While the assurance program along with its significantly lower effective tax rate encourages work and reduces welfare dependency, the $50 set-aside allows custodial family to stay on welfare longer by effectively loosening income eligibility by the amount of set-aside.

Table 5.4

Comparison of Three Public Child Support Plans, for Hypothetical Family of Three Receiving $160 per Month in Child Support

	AFDC Current System	CSA Wisconsin version	CAP New York version
Private payment	$160	$160	$160
Public guarantee[a]	$372	$223	$223
Custodial tax rate	0.67	0.25	0.10 [b]

Net wage = $4

Hours	Net earnings	Family income	Gov't cost	Family income	Gov't cost	Family income	Gov't cost
0	$ 0	$422	$262	$223	$63	$223	$63
40	160	475	155	343	23	367	47
80	320	528	49	480	0	511	31
120	480	640	0	640	0	655	15
160	640	800	0	800	0	800	0

Net wage = $6

Hours	Net earnings	Family income	Gov't cost	Family income	Gov't cost	Family income	Gov't cost
0	$ 0	$422	$262	$223	$63	$223	$63
40	240	502	102	403	3	439	39
80	480	640	0	640	0	655	15
120	720	880	0	880	0	880	0
160	960	1,120	0	1,120	0	1,120	0

[a]   AFDC guarantee is set at the median among all states for 1992. CSA and CAP guarantees are set at 60% of AFDC guarantee.

[b]   Custodial tax rate in CAP is set at 10% for earnings below poverty, and 67% for earnings above. The higher rate is not effective in any of the scenarios here.

Therefore the set-aside actually makes welfare and non-work more attractive.

A similar effect is inherent in the approach of CAP. While the earnings incentives on CAP are substantially higher than either AFDC or CSA, the incentives exist only as long as the custodial family remains in poverty. In addition, since eligibility for CAP is based on welfare, it does not remove the stigma of being dependent on an unpopular welfare program. It also creates the adverse incentives of potentially encouraging custodial families to join welfare in order to get on CAP.

The time is perhaps ripe for a new type of public financing of child support. During the 102nd Congress, Senator Dale Bumpass introduced a measure that would give custodial parents a tax credit for delinquent child support payments.[21] Such a measure would be equivalent to a small public child support benefit program with an individualized guarantee in the form of a tax credit. The guarantee would be set at the same proportion of the private support award as the custodial family's marginal income tax rate. Although this proposal provides a public financial protection without adversely affecting work effort, the measure has two shortcomings. It leaves out the truly low-income custodial families who do not pay taxes. In addition, a tax credit at the end of the tax year does not serve as a buffer against irregular support payments.

In contrast, the Downey-Hyde proposal, also unveiled in the 102nd Congress, calls for a child support assurance with a uniform benefit level financed by the federal government. This proposal is certain to emerge again in the coming sessions of Congress. And we will revisit the issues involved in setting up a national child support assurance program in the last chapter of the book.

Notes for Chapter 5

1. Donald T. Oellerich, Irwin Garfinkel, and Philip K. Robins, "Private Child Support: Current and Potential Impacts," *Journal of Sociology and Social Welfare* 18 (1991): 3-23. The child support guidelines used in that study are the Wisconsin and Colorado guidelines.

2. Irwin Garfinkel and Annette Sorensen, "Sweden's Child Support System: Lessons for the United States," *Social Work* 27 (1982): 509-513. Irwin Garfinkel and Pat Wong, "Child Support and Public Policy," in *Lone-Parent Families: The Economic Challenge* (Paris: Organization for Economic Cooperation and Development, 1990).

3. Irwin Garfinkel, "Child Support Assurance: A New Tool for Achieving Social Security," in Alfred J. Kahn and Sheila B. Kamerman, *Child Support: From Debt Collection to Social Policy* (Newbury Park: Sage, 1988); Irwin Garfinkel and Sara S. McLanahan, *Single Mothers and Their Children* (Urban Institute, 1986), pp. 181-183.

4. *The Green Book, 1992*, p.639.

5. As mentioned earlier, the assurance benefit has to be lower than the AFDC benefit to maintain the same cost in benefit payments. This is also consistent with the notion that child support assurance is designed to provide for the children but not the custodial parent.

6. Thomas Corbett, "The Wisconsin Child Support Assurance System: From Plausible Proposals to Improbable Prospects," in Irwin Garfinkel, Sara S. McLanahan, and Philip K. Robins, eds., *Child Support Assurance: Design Issues, Expected Impacts, and Political Barriers as Seen from Wisconsin* (Washington, DC: Urban Institute Press, 1992).

7. *Ibid.*, p.44.

6. Wisconsin is a high AFDC-benefit state. The level of CSA is deliberately set below the AFDC benefits for cost containment reason. A low level of assurance benefit also minimizes the income effect that tends to discourage work among non-welfare custodial parents. See Ann

Nichols-Casebolt, Irwin Garfinkel, and Pat Wong, "Reforming Wisconsin's Child Support System," in Sheldon Danziger and John F. Witte, eds., *State Policy Choices: The Wisconsin Experience* (Madison, WI: University of Wisconsin Press, 1988).

9. See, for example, Stanley Masters and Irwin Garfinkel, *Estimating Labor Supply Effects of Income Maintenance Alternatives* (New York NY: Academic Press, 1978), especially pp. 154-175.

10. See Pat Wong, *The Economic Effects of the Wisconsin Child Support Assurance System: A Simulation Study with a Labor Supply Model* (Madison, WI: University of Wisconsin unpublished dissertation, 1988).

11. For more details of the results, see Irwin Garfinkel, Philip K. Robins, Pat Wong, and Daniel R. Meyer, "The Wisconsin Child Support Assurance System: Estimated Effects on Poverty, Labor Supply, Caseloads, and Costs." *Journal of Human Resources* 25 (1990): 1-31.

12. The sample is derived from two sources: non-AFDC families (N = 242) are from a survey of Wisconsin Children, Income, and Program Participation; AFDC families (N = 4,735) are from the Wisconsin Computer Reporting Network, the administrative information system of AFDC cases in the State of Wisconsin. These cases are weighed to reflect the correct proportion of welfare status in the state.

13. The improvement is estimated probabilistically based on individual characteristics. At the aggregate level, the medium improvement corresponds to changing the rate of child support award to about 75 percent for divorced custodial parents, from a baseline level of 60 percent as reported in the data; for never-married custodial parents, the overall rate changes to 70 percent from a current level of 40 percent. In terms of collection, the aggregate change in the medium improvement scenario is from a baseline level of 63 percent of collection to about 82 percent.

14. Daniel R. Meyer, Irwin Garfinkel, Donald T. Oellerich, and Philip K. Robin, "Who Should be Eligible for an Assured Child Support Benefit?" in Irwin Garfin-

kel, Sara S. McLanahan, and Philip K. Robin, eds., *Child Support Assurance: Design Issues, Expected Impacts, and Political Barriers as Seen from Wisconsin* (Washington, DC: Urban Institute Press, 1992).

15. The data set is from U.S. Bureau of Census, Current Population Survey, Child Support Supplement collected in April of 1986.

16. New York State Task Force on Poverty and Welfare, *A New Social Contract: Rethinking the Nature and Purpose of Public Assistance* (December, 1986): 98-99.

17. In 1992, CAP is operating as a demonstration project in seven counties in New York State. In Albany, Allegheny, Chautauqua, and Ulster Counties, enrollment is open to all AFDC families with child support order. In Monroe, Niagara, and Suffolk Counties, enrollment is on a random assignment basis to allow for the comparison between the experimental and the control groups.

18. *The Green Book*, 1992, P.646.

19. William L. Hamilton, Nancy R. Burnstein, Elizabeth Davis, and Margaret Hargreaves, *The New York Child Assistance Program: Interim Report on Program Impacts* (Cambridge MA: Abt Associates, 1992).

20. The Wisconsin proposal of $3,000 is equivalent to about 55% of that state's AFDC guarantee. New York's program sets benefit level at two-thirds of that of its regular AFDC program.

21. Senator Bumpass's proposal, S.2514, was added as an amendment to H.R.11, the urban aid bill, which was eventually vetoed by President Bush.

6

Supporting Parental Employment

Child support assurance is a sensible way to provide an income floor without creating insurmountable disincentives to work. The assurance symbolizes the public's obligation to children growing up with only one parent at home. This income floor by itself is not intended to provide for all the economic needs of the children, however. Quite the contrary, in order for the assurance benefit to be available to as many custodial families as possible, the assurance level must be set at a relatively low level to be fiscally manageable. The income from the assurance program must therefore be supplemented by other resources. The most obvious resource is the custodial parent's earnings. This reflects the economic reality as well as the public's expectation of mutual reciprocity.

The fact remains that many custodial parents have very low market wage rate because of their limited education or work experience.[1] Recent analysis by the General Accounting Office shows that 35 percent of all currently single mothers in poverty would still be poor even if they had worked full-time for an entire year.[2] In order for a mother with two children to reach the 1992 federal poverty level of $11,280 on earnings alone, she would have to work full-time at about $5.50 an hour. A single mother of three would have to earn $7.00 per hour to reach the poverty line of $14,463. Taking into account expenses incidental to work and absenteeism because of child illness, even poverty living standard may be out of reach for many of these custodial families.

The prospects for single mothers to climb out of poverty through earnings have become dimmer over the years. In 1988, almost 17 percent of single mothers with children under six who worked full-time year-round were still in poverty. That proportion was up from 10 percent in 1980. Among the custodial mothers who worked only part-time, the poverty rate went up to 60 percent in 1988, up from 51 percent in 1980.[3]

Thus working at the market wage would not provide a self-sufficient level of income for custodial parents with low earnings capacity. The income would not be sufficient even in the presence of a child support assurance. As discussed in the last chapter, nationwide simulation results demonstrate that an assurance level of $2,000 per year would lead to a 24 percent rise in work hours by AFDC custodial parents, a rather small amount since the level of employment among AFDC recipients is very low to begin with. In 1990 fewer than 7 percent of the custodial mothers on AFDC worked full-time or part-time.[4]

Besides low wages, custodial parents face the dilemma of being the sole breadwinner and the homemaker at the same time. Tremendous barriers exist against their efforts to work off AFDC. Child care and health insurance top the list of these barriers. Benefits, in cash or in kind, may help to some extent, but other barriers are more psychological and can only be overcome by a social support network.

This chapter considers government strategies in providing a support structure to make work feasible and economically rewarding. This is the last dimension in the framework for child support policy identified in chapter 3, but it certainly is not the least important. One strategy to provide such a support structure would be to expand the provision of basic social services. Another strategy would be to enhance the reward of work by directly subsidizing the take-home pay of custodial parents.

Services in Support of Employment

For both budgetary and political reasons, in-kind services to support custodial parent employment are more popular among the public than expenditures on cash benefits. The Family Support Act contains such service provisions through the Job Opportunities and Basic Skills (JOBS) program, and state-provided child care for AFDC parents who work or participate in JOBS, as well as through transitional child care and medicaid coverage for parents leaving AFDC because of earnings increase.

The Family Support Act represents a beginning step in a new direction of the work strategy to welfare reform.[5] In addition to *requiring* work as earlier legislation did, the notion of *supporting* work is reflected in the mandates for child care services and coverage during the transition to self-sufficiency. It is a recognition of the need for a comprehensive infrastructure of services in order for custodial families to attain and maintain their self-sufficiency.

However, there is no reason to restrict the public's role to serving custodial parents already receiving public child support. The infrastructure of support should also help noncustodial parents to discharge their financial obligations through better employment prospects and likewise help prevent non-welfare custodial parents from having to rely on AFDC.

Noncustodial parent programs

The public role in employment support for noncustodial parents is a new development. Currently two demonstration projects are underway. The Parents Fair Share project, jointly sponsored by the federal government and philanthropies, enrolls unemployed noncustodial parents into JOBS programs in selected states. The demonstration project will determine whether job search, skills training, and peer support from JOBS would have an impact on noncustodial parents' payment of child support as well as on their relationship with the children.

Another on-going project targets unwed fathers. Funded by the Mott Foundation and carried out by Public/Private Ventures, the Young Unwed Fathers Demonstration works with local employers in six communities to place unwed noncustodial fathers eligible for Job Training Partnership Act in training and employment positions. The project also provides education to the fathers through its fatherhood curriculum which emphasizes parenting skills and parental responsibility.

Child care and health insurance

Besides providing employment support services for individuals already on welfare, there is also a strong argument for some type of preventive measures. Services ought to be made available to custodial parents who are not currently on public assistance but who are at risk of being so. The Omnibus Budget Reconciliation Act of 1990 authorized the at-risk child care program to address this issue. Funds are available as federal matching monies to state allocations. Individual recipients must be from low-income families who are not on AFDC but would become eligible if child care services are unavailable. Under this program, states are allowed to charge fees on a sliding scale.

Another important element of this support network is health care coverage. Since a custodial family's eligibility for medicaid is contingent upon participation in AFDC, leaving AFDC through work may mean losing health coverage if there is no health benefits provided by the employer. It is estimated that, had eligibility for Medicaid been dissociated from AFDC status, as many as 10 percent of custodial families would leave AFDC.[6]

The most effective way of removing health coverage as an impediment to work is therefore a government-sponsored health insurance program covering all children.

This, however, involves the broader policy issue of national health care reform. Short of such a program, the current child support system requires, under the 1984 amendments to the Social Security Act, that medical support be included as part of a private child support award as long as such insurance is available to the noncustodial parent at reasonable cost. In practice, however, most states do not have an adequate administrative mechanism to enforce this provision.[7] In addition, the Employee Retirement Income and Security Act (ERISA) allows health insurance plans to exclude coverage of nonresident dependents. Consequently, children often are not covered by the insurance policy of the noncustodial parents.

Family Support Programs

Some custodial parents are in need of more than child care and medical coverage. Before a custodial parent can take up a job outside the home, issues within the home need to be addressed. The absence of one parent means that the custodial parent needs to shoulder all the responsibilities of child rearing from household chores to psychological stress. This burden is often exacerbated when the custodial family has inadequate financial resources. Research indicates that single parenthood often leads to lower achievement level of the children.[8] These families are also at higher risk of developing a wide range of family problems, including the perpetuation of welfare dependency.[9]

In order to assist these families on their path to self-sufficiency, child support policy must provide family-focused services to strengthen these families. These services should be preventive in nature and be available at an early point of the family's entrance into the child support system. As Isabel Sawhill, senior fellow at the Urban Institute, testified in a Congressional hearing,

> I have become convinced that one reason we have not made more progress in reducing poverty is because we have spent too

much on alleviating the symptoms of poverty and not enough on
prevention. At the heart of a prevention strategy, in my view,
is more attention to the needs of children and their families. Put
simply, if we are to break the cycle of poverty, we must inter-
vene early.[10]

In response to the need of early intervention of
families at risk, the notion of family support programs has
emerged over the past decade. Based on research evidence
on comprehensive and preventive services to at-risk
families, family support programs represent a movement
against the traditional, ameliorative, categorical services
targeted at individual family members.[11] A typical
family support program would include several of the
following services: parent education and support groups;
parent-child activities focusing on child development;
family life education; drop-in center with staff support;
child care during program activities; information and
referral to other community services; home visits; and
health and nutritional screening.[12]

The need for family support services was formally
endorsed by Congress in the Comprehensive Child Development Act of 1988 (P.L.100-297). This legislation authorized up to 25 local demonstration projects that incorporate three objectives: preventing educational failure of the
young by addressing the psychological, medical, and social
needs of infants and young children; decreasing the
likelihood that young children are caught in the cycle of
poverty; and preventing welfare dependency and promoting self-sufficiency.

To qualify for funding as a demonstration project, a
local program must set up a management information
system and individual case management plans on participants; provide developmental screening and early intervention for children; involve parents in literacy education,
vocational training, and parenting skills; and make health
care accessible to participants. These requirements are
intended to steer local service agencies in the direction of
setting up a network of collaborative, integrated services
for the entire family.[13]

Since the purpose of the legislation is to set up demonstration projects, its scale remains relatively small. In the 1992 fiscal year, actual appropriations for the program were $45 million, providing funds for 24 projects. Despite its limited scale, P.L.100-297 signals a step toward an important direction.

Revival of the service strategy

Single-parent families, especially those that have experienced long cycle of poverty and welfare dependency, are among the most vulnerable to other family problems. For some of them, no amount of child support assurance could be sufficient to break through the entrenchment in the cycle of dependency. An earlier era of service strategy, exemplified by the counseling programs in the 1962 amendment to the Social Security Act, tended to focus on individual adequacy and isolated problems perceived to affect job readiness. As the work strategy turned from counseling and incentives to work requirement, the service strategy went out of favor.

The service strategy has become an important element of welfare reform again, only this time it resurfaces with the realization that it is the services coordinated to match the needs of the entire family unit that are successful.[14] While the establishment of a comprehensive service strategy to serve custodial families at risk will undoubtedly be time-consuming, the ultimate objective should be to decategorize the existing system of funding for family services so that local services can be delivered in a more flexible manner to enable a holistic approach to fit family needs.

The ultimate preventive strategy in the child support system is to strengthen the family unit and to reduce the number of marital disruption and nonmarital birth, so that fewer children would enter the child support system and become in need of intensive services. Unfortunately little has been done in the current system to serve low-income two-parent families on a preventive basis.

Supplementing Earnings

One federal program does intend to strengthen two-parent families as well as those headed by a single parent.[15] The earned income tax credit (EITC) is operated as an earnings subsidy program within the federal income tax structure. EITC provides a refundable tax credit to all *working* low-income families with children.

The credit is "phased in" as a constant percentage of earnings from the first dollar of earned wages and up to an earnings ceiling. To avoid subsidizing families with higher incomes, the credit is phased out, or taken back, again as a percentage of earned income, beginning at an income level above the phase-in ceiling. The credit offsets the family's federal income tax liability. Any remaining credit after the offset is refundable.

To illustrate how EITC works, we will take 1975, the first year of the program, as an example. The phase-in rate in 1975 was at 10 percent regardless of the number of children. The credit was available up to a family income ceiling of $4,000 that year. As shown in Table 6.1, this amounted to a maximum credit of $400. Above income level of $4,000, the credit was phased out again at ten cents for each dollar of earnings, until eligibility for the credit disappeared at $8,000 of income.

Over the years the allowed credits have been made more generous through periodic changes in phase-in and phase-out rates, as well as in phase-in ceiling and the income level at which the credit begins to phase out. Because of inflation, however, the real level of benefits had hardly increased until the most recent and significant change in 1990.

As part of the Omnibus Budget Reconciliation Act of that year, slightly higher rates were established for both phase-in and phase-out for families with two or more children, and eligible income levels were raised and indexed to inflation.

Table 6.1

Earned Income Tax Credit Program Structure
Selected Years

Year	Phase-in		Maximum	Phase-Out		
	Rate	Ceiling	Credit	Rate	Floor	Ending Income
1975	10.0%	$4,000	$ 400	10.00%	$4,000	$ 8,000
1978	10.0	5,000	500	12.50	4,000	10,000
1981	10.0	5,000	500	12.50	6,000	10,000
1985	11.0	5,000	550	12.22	6,500	11,000
1987	14.0	6,080	851	10.00	6,920	15,432
1989	14.0	6,500	910	10.00	10,240	19,340
1991	16.7[a]	7,140	1,192	11.93	11,250	21,250
	17.3[b]	7,140	1.235	12.36	11,250	21,250
1992	17.6[a]	7,520	1,324	12.57	11,840	22,370
	18.4[b]	7,500	1,324	13.14	11,840	22,370

[a] Program parameters for families with one child.
[b] Program parameters for families with two children.
Source: U.S. House of Representatives, Committee on Ways and Means, Overview of Entitlement Programs: *1992 Green Book.*

The coverage of EITC is certainly broader than families in the child support system alone, but its rationale does serve as an important model for public support of custodial parent employment. EITC can be thought of as a bonus to encourage work in low-income families, it can also be thought of as the public's contribution towards overcoming barriers to work, such as child care expenses.[16]

Although the annual amount of benefit is not large in absolute terms, EITC boosts the income of most working custodial families who live below poverty by almost one-fifth in 1992. For example, a parent working full-time at the minimum wage makes about $8,840 in 1992. If she receives $2,000 in private child support or from assurance payment, she would still be eligible for the maximum credit of $1,324 in EITC since her total income is still below the phase-out floor of $11,840. This credit is enough to bring her pre-tax income to slightly above the poverty level for a family of three.

Potential extensions

Since EITC is available to all families with children, it provides the same benefits for low-income noncustodial parents with children from a new marriage as it does for custodial families. This concept can be extended to provide earnings incentives to low-income noncustodial parents to induce increased payment of private child support. The idea of making parents who pay child support eligible for the Earned Income Tax Credit--without residing with the child--has been proposed.[17]

Such a program would be equivalent to a small public child support benefit provided specifically as a matching payment for private child support. Since the matching payments from the government would go to the noncustodial parents, this program, if implemented, would not increase the amounts received by the children. It would, however, lessen the burden to, and hopefully increase the likelihood of child support payment by, low-income noncustodial parents. The program predicates noncustodial parent eligibility on both working and discharging full child support responsibility. In that regard, it is a measure embodying the idea of mutual reciprocity.

EITC can also be modified to provide more generous tax credits to custodial parents. For instance, a higher phase-in rate can be provided for custodial families only. Under the current income tax structure, single heads of household enjoy a higher standard deduction than single individuals and married couples. The same break can be extended to EITC to express society's support of custodial parent employment.

Making an existing, general program more generous for a special group is bound to be politically difficult. This is especially true when that group has traditionally been associated with welfare. EITC was established as one of the few financial assistance programs with eligibility for both two-parent and one-parent families. It would seem politically advisable to keep it that way. More importantly, an additional EITC-like benefit would not be a cost-efficient way of assisting custodial families.

Since EITC provides a constant rate of benefit in proportion to earnings up to the phase-in maximum, the result is to give more benefits in absolute terms to families with relatively more earnings. Referring back to Table 6.1, families with adjusted gross income between $7,500 and $11,840 in 1992 would get the highest amount of credit, $1,324 for one child. For the general population, this range covers families in the lower end of the family income distribution. That is, families who obtain the maximum credit are relatively disadvantaged compared to all families with children.

Among families headed by a custodial parent, however, an income of $12,000 is close to the median in 1992. Custodial families who can take the best advantage of the current EITC structure, therefore, are those in the middle income range rather than the most needy ones. Of course this is not to say that custodial families in the middle income range do not need support. It nevertheless indicates that if additional but limited resources are targeted at the population of custodial families, the ceiling of the phase-in range should be made relatively low even as an additional credit rate is applied. This would make EITC unnecessarily complicated and even less politically feasible.

In addition, since EITC is an earnings subsidy, it provides equal benefits to a higher-wage individual working fewer hours and a lower-wage individual working longer hours. If the purpose of public support is to encourage custodial parents with low skills to work off welfare, it would be advisable to design a program that concentrates support on the latter group. In this regard, a wage subsidy is a better device.

Custodial Parent Wage Subsidy

If low wage rate and high work expenses are the reasons custodial parents often do not earn enough to make working worthwhile, subsidizing their wage rate seems to be a direct solution. Wage subsidies targeted at custodial parents are justified since child care is not optional for working single parents. Wage subsidies can be thought of as a child care subsidy if encouraging work is an objective. This idea was incorporated into some versions of the Wisconsin Child Support Assurance System research.[18]

While child care costs vary a great deal depending on the type of care and geographic location, the average cost was around $1.50 per hour per child.[19] The notion of a work expense offset (WEO) was included in some versions of the Wisconsin CSAS simulation studies to reflect this cost.

Work expense offset

Under WEO, a non-AFDC custodial parent with a child support award would receive, in addition to child support assurance, an "offset" of $1.00 per hour of work for one child, and $1.75 per hour for two or more children. Again to control cost, several features are built into the program to restrict eligibility. First, there is a limit on the maximum amount of WEO per family per year. This limit was set at $2,000. For a custodial parent with two children, this maximum is reached when she has worked 1,143 hours, or slightly more than half-time a year.

Second, WEO is provided only to non-AFDC custodial families with relatively low income, with a phase out mechanism similar to EITC. In the phase-out range for WEO, a surtax is imposed so that all public child support benefits--CSA as well as WEO--would be recovered at $2,000 below Wisconsin's median income for families with the same number of children.[20] The ceiling for the WEO phase-in range is set at half of the income level at which WEO is totally phased out.

For instance, if the median income for families with two children in Wisconsin is $22,000, then a custodial family with two children would be eligible for the hourly WEO until the family reaches an income of $10,000. Beyond this income level, her additional earnings would be taxed at a rate such that, by the time the family reaches the income of $20,000, all assurance benefits and work expense offsets would have been repaid to the government. Naturally, at this point the surtax is removed. This feature creates significant work incentives for families with income below half the median family income. It also implies that public support is deemed unnecessary for custodial families with income close to the state median.

WEO in effect increases the wage rate of a low-income custodial parent by somewhere between one-quarter to one-half.[21] As demonstrated in Figure 6.1, in the absence of an assurance benefit, WEO alone would increase the slope of the budget line CD, which represents earnings and private child support only. Since WEO is offered to accompany child support assurance in the Wisconsin proposal, the effective budget option of the CSA-WEO program becomes the line segments BHE.

BK has a steeper slope than CD since it represents the phase-in range of the work expense offset program. In this range the effective wage rate is equal to the market wage rate of the custodial parent, plus the work expense subsidy. The effect of the steeper slope is to allow the total income along BK to exceed the total income along AF (the welfare option) at an even lower number of work hours than in the previous CSA-only program [See Figure 5.1]. The vertical distance KH_k represents the phase-in income ceiling for WEO. Beyond K, the segment KE takes over. It has a flatter slope because of the custodial tax now imposed to phase out of both CSA and WEO. At the income level equivalent to EH_3, all CSA and WEO benefits disappear.

The larger the difference between the benefit guarantee of AFDC and child support assurance, the more important the wage incentives are in encouraging the custodial parents to choose the non-AFDC option. If the assurance TB is very close to TA, for example, a regular market wage rate would result in the non-AFDC budget line BE intersecting the AFDC budget line AF at a very low level of work effort, making leaving welfare relatively easy. Thus, WEO is specially important for states with high AFDC benefits like Wisconsin.

Impact assessment

WEO is a significant incentive to work for custodial parents on welfare, as indicated by the results of simulation in Wisconsin when the CSA-WEO program is incorporated into the CSAS proposal. In chapter 5, the following impacts of the CSA program are predicted for an assurance level of $3,000 per year: $20 million savings in Wisconsin's public child support system, 3 percent reduction in AFDC caseload, and 16 percent reduction in

Figure 6.1
Wisconsin CSAS, with Work Expense Offset
in addition to CSA

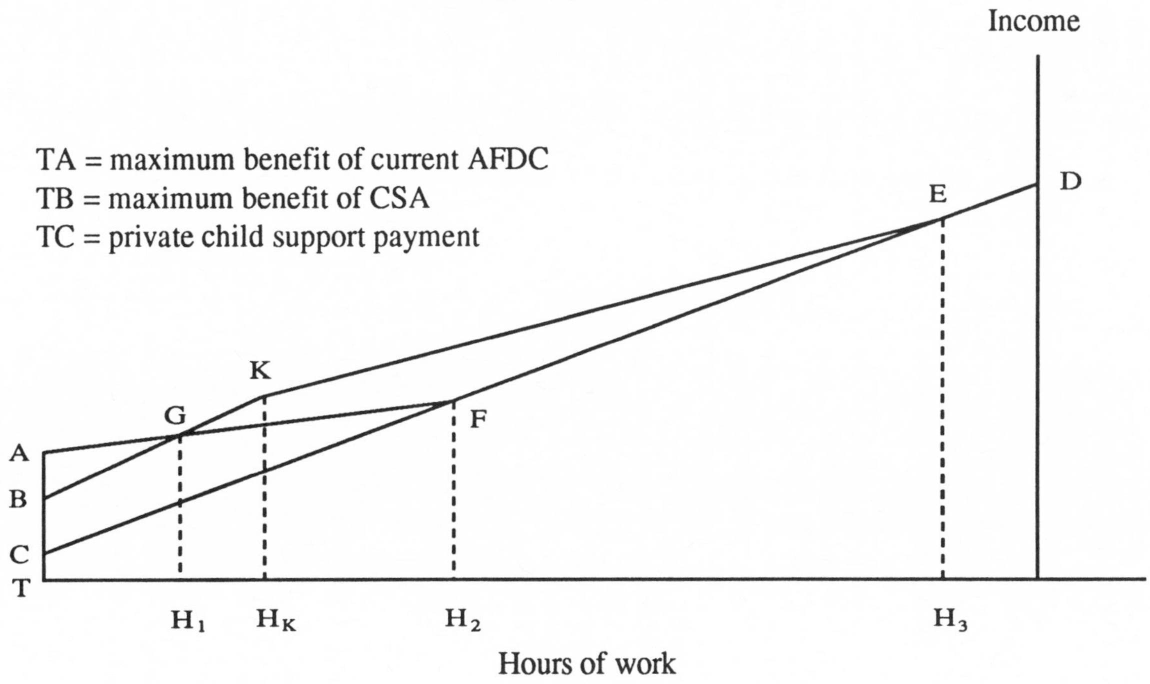
Income
TA = maximum benefit of current AFDC
TB = maximum benefit of CSA
TC = private child support payment
D
E
K
G
F
A
B
C
T
H_1
H_K
H_2
H_3
Hours of work

poverty gap, with an increase of 16 percent in work hours by parents currently on welfare. These results are reproduced in the first row of Table 6.2.

When WEO is added to a CSA benefit of $3,000, net savings are cut by one-half, to $10 million. AFDC caseload and poverty gap reduction are predicted to be 8 percent and 18 percent respectively, and current AFDC recipients are expected to increase their work hours by 66 percent. Since the addition of WEO boosts AFDC reduction by almost three times and work effort of welfare recipients by an even higher proportion, it is clear that current AFDC recipients respond to the work incentives in WEO more favorably than they do to those in CSA.

If a WEO program is available, a reduction in the level of assurance benefit may be appropriate. The simulated impacts of an assurance benefit of $2,000 are presented in the third row. Those numbers indicate a level of AFDC reduction rate much closer to the 3 percent level achieved by a CSA of $3,000 without a WEO. At the same time total savings would be $15 million, half-way between the savings resulting from a CSA of $3,000 alone and from a CSA of $3,000 plus the WEO program.

These simulation results, based on Wisconsin data, again show that the combination of child support assurance and work expense offset result in a modest level of welfare reduction and would not cost any more than the current AFDC system if private support enforcement is at all close to the projected medium level of improvement. One limitation of this analysis, of course, is that the simulation model predicts the choice of the custodial parents under the proposed reform, without taking into account conditions in the larger economic environment. To the extent that the availability of jobs is a factor preventing custodial families from gaining economic independence, assurance benefits or work subsidies would not be sufficient assistance. Nonetheless, the simulation results clearly show that these new programs are tools for enforcing both public responsibility for children and parental

Table 6.2

Estimated Combined Effects of Child Support Assurance and Work Expense Offset, Wisconsin, 1985[a]

| Scenario[b] | Net Savings[c] ($ Millions) | % Reduction in AFDC Caseload | % Reduction in Poverty Gap | % Change in Hours of Work | | |
				AFDC Families	Non-AFDC Families	All Families
CSA ($3,000) only	$20	3%	16%	+16%	-4%	-1%
CSA ($3,000) and WEO	$10	8%	18%	+66%	-4%	0%
CSA ($2,000) and WEO	$15	4%	17%	+37%	-4%	-1%

[a] Percentages are calculated using averages before CSAS. Net savings are in millions of 1985 dollars.

[b] Scenarios are mutually exclusive.

[c] Savings are based on changes in AFDC and CSA expenditures, as well as changes in income tax revenues resulting from differences in earnings, before and after the CSAS system is in place.

Source: Irwin Garfinkel, Philip K. Robins, Pat Wong, and Daniel R. Meyer, "The Wisconsin Child Support Assurance System: Estimated Effects on Poverty, Labor Supply, Caseload, and Costs," p.22.

obligation for self-sufficiency that would not place additional burden on taxpayers.

Thus far we have focused on the combined effects of a support assurance and wage subsidy on poverty and welfare caseload. However, the simulation results in Wisconsin also predict a mild reduction in work effort predicted among the non-welfare population of custodial parents. Table 6.2 indicates a 4 percent decrease in work hours with the implementation of CSAS. Is this a cause for concern?

Public Child Support and Dependency

The reduction in work among non-welfare custodial parents in the simulation is due mostly to the effect of the increase in private child support payments. It has very little to do with the availability of the new public support benefits. This is indicated by the fact that the improvements in the private system, in the absence of *any* child support assurance or work expense offset, would by themselves decrease work effort among non-welfare families by 3 percent (see Table 5.1). The addition of these new versions of public child support, therefore, adds just one percentage point to the decline. This decline is also unresponsive to the level or type of public support benefits. The work reduction level remains at 4 percent under every row in Table 6.1.

An examination of the nationwide result in Table 5.2 leads to the same conclusion. There improvements in private support policy alone would cut the labor supply of non-welfare custodial parents by 3 percent, but little additional decline is predicted as the assurance program is introduced and when the benefit level increases. Therefore there should be little concern that the reform in public child support, in the form of CSA or WEO, would lead to appreciable disincentive effects among custodial parents who are not currently on welfare.

Nonetheless one may be worried about the potential expansion of government benefits implied by these reform proposals. Even if these new programs do not cause a decrease in work effort, they do lead many non-welfare families to become part of the government benefit system, either through an assurance benefit or through work expense offset. Is such a trade-off worthwhile?

This boils down to the notion of *dependency on government* as a social problem. If one views the problem of dependency as the *number of families* receiving any public child support benefits at all, then the elements of the Wisconsin Child Support Assurance System do in fact increase dependency. A decomposition of the Wisconsin simulation result shows that, while before CSAS, 46 percent of the sample are dependent on AFDC receipts. That proportion rises to 56 percent when a CSA of $3,000 and the WEO are also available as government benefits. By this measure, government dependency has increased by one-fifth.

If, however, dependency is defined as the *magnitude of government benefits* received by the population, these public child support proposals have not increased dependency. The same decomposition of the Wisconsin results shows that, before CSAS, the average amount of government public child support received by the sample was $2,538 (in 1985 dollars). With a $3,000 CSA and WEO, the average amount of government benefits becomes $2,425. Viewed in this light, dependency has actually on average declined by around 4 percent.

Yet another way of thinking about dependency is to measure dependency ratio, or the proportion of total income of each family derived from government sources. The average income of the Wisconsin sample is $17,961 before the simulation. The simulation results show that it increases to $19,011 with the $3,000 CSA/WEO plan. The aggregate government dependency ratios are therefore 14.1 and 12.7 percent respectively, a decline of dependency of about one-tenth with the introduction of CSA and WEO.[22]

The decline in dependency, if measured by the magnitude of public benefit receipts, results from a larger decline in AFDC benefits than the increase in CSAS benefits. When dependency ratio is used as the measure, the decline in dependency is due additionally to the increase in private child support payment as part of family incomes. In any event, these alternative definitions of dependency are not inherently better or worse than the notion of dependency as receiving any government benefit. The proper indicator of problematic dependency is eventually a political issue, depending on the type of dependency to which society is the most averse.

There are inevitably political pressures to limit the magnitude of government expenditures as well as the caseload in benefit programs. However, these issues per se are not the central concern of politicians and the public. The social security program, for example, is a lot larger than the current public child support program, in terms of both expenditures and the number of beneficiaries. Yet few think of social security as creating a dependency problem in social policy.

As analysts of welfare reform from Charles Murray to Lawrence Mead to Daniel Patrick Moynihan would probably agree, the concern of the public is how *heavily* single-headed families become dependent on government assistance. Dependency becomes a problem when it is to such an extent that a individuals have lost any motivation to retain, or achieve, the self-sufficiency society expects of them. Retirees on social security can afford not to be self-sufficient because social norms do not expect them to be so.

On the other hand, non-aged widows or widowers with children under the survivors insurance program are expected to be self-sufficient. Since the survivors insurance benefits they receive are not means-tested and do not discourage work as much as AFDC does, widowed families are generally not heavily dependent upon benefits from government. Although survivors insurance benefits are more generous than AFDC, the aggregate dependency ratio among all survivors insurance recipient families is about 33 percent,[23] whereas the dependency ratio among all AFDC families in the Wisconsin sample of custodial families is 72 percent.

Although there may be demographic differences between the families on these two programs, it is likely that the differences in incentive structure between the two programs is just as important a reason for the disparity in dependency ratio. The reform of the public child support system incorporated in the Child Support Assurance System has sought to create a program structure similar to that of survivors insurance. This program structure emphasizes incentives for work so families can minimize their receipt of public benefits. This is essential for the restructuring of public child support, and that is why assurance benefits and work expense offsets are not merely alternative versions of welfare programs.

Notes for Chapter 6

1. Irwin Garfinkel and Sara S. McLanahan, *Single Mothers and Their Children: A New American Dilemma* (Washington, DC: Urban Institute Press, 1986).

2. U.S. General Accounting Office, *Mother-only Families: Low Earnings will Keep Many Children in Poverty*, GAO/HRD-91-62 (Washington, DC: GAO, April 1991).

3. U.S. General Accounting Office, *Poverty Trends, 1980-88: Changes in Family Composition and Income Sources among the Poor*, GAO/PEMD-92-34 (Washington, DC: GAO, September 1992).

4. U.S. House of Representatives, Committee on Ways and Means, *Overview of Entitlement Programs: 1992 Green Book* (Washington, DC: Government Printing Office, 1992).

5. Sheila Smith, Susan Blank, and Ray Collins, *Pathways to Self-Sufficiency for Two Generations: Designing Welfare-to-Work Programs that Benefit Children and Streng-*

then Families (New York, NY: Foundation for Child Development, 1992).

6. Robert Moffitt and Barbara Wolfe, "The Effect of the Medicaid Program on Welfare Participation and Labor Supply," National Bureau of Economic Research Working Paper No. 3286 (Cambridge, MA: 1990).

7. U.S. General Accounting Office, *Medicaid: Ensuring That Noncustodial Parents Provide Health Insurance Can Save Costs.* GA)/HRD-92-80 (Washington, DC: GAO, June 1992).

8. E. Mavis Hetherington, Kathleen A. Camara, and David L. Featherman, "Achievement and Intellectual Functioning of Children in One-Parent Households," in J. Spence, ed., *Achievement and Achievement Motives* (San Francisco, CA: W.H.Freeman, 1983).

9. Sara S. McLanahan and Irwin Garfinkel, "Single Mothers, the Underclass and Social Policy," *Annals of the American Academy of Political and Social Science* 501 (1989): 92-104.

10. Isabel V. Sawhill, "Toward More Integrated Services for Children: Issues and Options," Statement before the Subcommittee on Children, Family, Drugs, and Alcoholism, U.S. Senate Committee on Labor and Human Resources, May 7, 1991.

11. Sharon Kagan, George Powell, Bernice Weissbourd, and Edward Zigler, *America's Family Support Programs* (New Haven, CT: Yale University Press, 1987).

12. Bernice Weissbourd and Carol Emig, "Early Childhood Programs for Children in Poverty: A Good Place to Start," in George Miller, ed., *Giving Children a Chance: The Case for more Effective National Policies* (Lanham, MD: Center for National Policy Press, 1989).

13. U.S. Administration on Children, Youth and Families, Head Start Bureau, *Comprehensive Child Development Programs, a National Family Support Demonstration* (Washington, DC: Government Printing Office, 1992).

14. Olivia Golden, *Poor Children and Welfare Reform* (Westport, CT: Auburn House, 1992).

15. Another major program available to two-parent families is food stamp. Instead of strengthening families by encouraging work, however, food stamp has the same work disincentive features as the existing AFDC program.

16. Eugene Steuerle and Paul Wilson, "The Earned Income Tax Credit" *Focus* 10 (1987): 1-8.

17. Laurie Bassi and Robert Lerman, "Incentive Effects of Child Support Payments: Essential Components for a Demonstration" (Unpublished paper, 1990).

18. Irwin Garfinkel, Philip K. Robins, Pat Wong, and Daniel R. Meyer, "The Wisconsin Child Support Assurance System: Estimated Effects on Poverty, Labor Supply, Caseloads, and Costs" *Journal of Human Resources* 25(1990): 1-31.

19. Sandra L. Hofferth, April Brayfield, Sharon Deich, and Pamela Holcomb, *National Child Care Survey, 1990* (Washington: Urban Institute Press, 1991), p.135.

20. In 1985, the median family incomes were $17,328 for families with one child and $21,372 for families with two children.

21. The minimum wage was $3.60 per hour when the work expense offset component was first considered in the Wisconsin CSAS reform.

22. An alternative measure would be the average of individual dependency ratio, which turns out to be 39% before and 38% after the simulation.

23. Martha N. Ozawa and William T. Alpert, "Distributive Effects of Survivors Insurance Benefits and Public Assistance," *Social Service Review* 58 (1984): 603-621.

7

A Model for the Future

A perennial issue in the design of social policy is whether programs should be universal or targeted to economic needs. Advocates of universalism argue that broad-based programs are more politically viable, less distortionary of economic behavior, and in fact more effective in aiding the truly needy.[1] On the other side of the debate, targeted programs are seen as more realistic during a period of budgetary retrenchment.[2] In particular, Robert Greenstein, defending the targeting approach in anti-poverty programs, argues that targeted programs are as politically strong and economically effective as universal programs as long as they are perceived by the public to be *earned* and are not narrowly restricted to "the poorest elements in society."[3] The earned income tax credit is an example of a popular targeted program that embodies both features.

The distinction between universal versus targeted coverage is also an important issue in envisioning the future child support system. Within the dual nature of the system, child support policy has historically been based on the distinction between public and private support, or equivalently between welfare and non-welfare status. Private support enforcement, which used to belong entirely to the judicial realm, entailed a set of operating rules and assumptions very different from those for public child support, the jurisdiction of "IV-A." Within that judicially-based system, there was to be no federal intervention into the life of families outside IV-A jurisdiction; noncustodial parents from these families were assumed to be responsible persons, able to discharge their support obligations voluntarily; custodial parents from these families were entitled to their privacy even if they sought government help in enforcing private support. For families on IV-A, the opposite was true in each case.

In practice this distinction began to blur with the bureaucratization of child support enforcement. That process made administrative enforcement services available to non-welfare families who so desired. Today welfare and non-welfare cases are covered by the same rules in some child support enforcement functions, like how awards are initially set and routinely collected.

Nevertheless the underlying policy design has not moved away from a paradigm using participation in public child support as the organizing theme. Mandatory parentage establishment to this day applies only to AFDC cases. Participation in IV-D continues to be voluntary for non-welfare families, as is the need for triennial review of award. The administration and evaluation of IV-D programs both emphasize the distinction between AFDC and non-AFDC collections. In a way this is only natural, for the child support system has retained its traditional distinction between financing through IV-A and enforcing the system through IV-D.

In addition to stigmatizing the portion of child-support-eligible population relying on public support, the distinction between private and public support is not effective in implementing mutual reciprocities among the noncustodial parent, the custodial parent, and the public, as too many non-AFDC child support cases fall through the cracks under such an approach.

An Integrated System

The concept of universal and targeted coverage offers an opportunity to integrate the dual system of child support. The proposal is a simple one: instead of organizing child support policy according to welfare status, a better design of the system would be based on the extent to which a particular child support function ought to be routinized and therefore universalized.

Child support functions fall into one of five elements identified in the normative policy framework: parentage establishment, award determination, collection, public financial protection, and infrastructure support. In chapter 4, it is recommended that a number of enforcement functions--collection by routine withholding and preliminary adjustment of awards--should be automated and federalized. Other functions, like parentage acknowledgement and the appeals process in award adjustment, can be handled by highly standardized guidelines but inevitably involve a discretionary dimension. These functions should remain the prerogatives of the states because of the intricate connections between these functions and other issues in family law.

These enforcement functions should continue to constitute the core activities of the nation's child support system, and they should be available universally, indeed, in a mandatory manner, to *all* custodial families. The appeal of universal coverage is that it upholds the tax liability model of child support obligations. Uniform treatment symbolizes the importance of parental obligations regardless of circumstances. All noncustodial parents would be held accountable, and all custodial families would be served by the enforcement system regardless of income or eligibility for public child support.

Universal coverage in these enforcement functions is also a sound policy economically. The preventive nature of these routinized procedures would reduce the need for the remedial pursuit of child support obligations later. Even if a custodial family is not currently on AFDC, child support enforcement on its behalf serves to avert the need to depend on public support. The resulting "cost avoidance" for the public is well worth the cost of service since the expense of serving an additional family in a routinized system is small.

Targeted Enforcement Services

It is quite another story when the services involved are costly. Some enforcement functions, notably the location of noncustodial parents and collection of arrearages, do not lend themselves to standardized procedures. These activities absorb a great deal of agency resources. A system of child support with limited resources cannot afford to serve all families in these activities. It is especially troubling if an enforcement agency with limited resources concentrates on providing such services free of charge to families that can, by and large, afford to pay for those services in part or in whole.

Unfortunately, that is where many state child support enforcement agencies find themselves today. The enforcement system has been set up with a built-in bias in favor of middle-class custodial families, at the expense of those who are on AFDC. Every custodial parent seeking services, say on collecting past due child support, from IV-D could obtain practically free services.[4] Federal incentive payments reward states for non-AFDC collections at the same rate as collections on behalf of welfare families.[5] Equal rate of incentive payments means that collecting back-support on behalf of non-AFDC cases is a better *investment* of state agency resources with respect to federal payments because, on average, the amount that could be collected from a non-welfare case is larger.

The net result is that enforcement resources are diverted to custodial families that are not in as much need. Since the child support collected for non-AFDC families belong to the families themselves, taxpayers benefit only in terms of AFDC cost avoidance, but not actual reduction in government expenditures or AFDC caseload. While preventing custodial families from having to go on AFDC is a worthwhile mission when the administrative cost is low, it is not necessarily the best use of agency resources when AFDC cases get piled up unserved as a result.

A policy choice has to be made. A solution to this problem is to charge custodial families above a certain income a fee for non-routine services such as collection of arrearages. The fee could be a certain percentage of the collected amount, but it should be substantial rather than nominal. This ensures that custodial families with the means would pay for the cost of the services. State revenues and federal funds would then finance the non-routine services exclusively for low-income families.

In fact, current federal regulations allow states to recover the actual costs of services on behalf of non-AFDC cases, either from the noncustodial or the custodial parent, after current support has been collected. This option is generally ignored by the states, however, because the expenditures recovered through this process would not be eligible for federal matching funds for program administration, which is currently at 66 percent of total administrative costs. In other words, from the perspective of a state agency, each dollar of collection cost charged to the family nets only 34 cents plus the baggage of political grief from local constituents that states would rather do without. Federal leadership in making this fee a mandate would therefore be a necessary step.

Targeting non-routine services at low-income families raises two issues. The first is what practical effect we might expect of it. The second is whether it is fair. Charging a fee for non-routine services would not in itself redirect the relative priorities currently allotted to non-welfare cases and welfare cases. Agencies would still have the incentives to cream off on cases with better economic background. However, the fee would have another, very important effect.

Public-private partnership

In addition to being reimbursement to the government--which the fee may well do--the fee serves a more important function, from the perspective of system design, as a device to ration government services. For-profit child support collection agencies have recently sprung up all across the country. While some agencies obtain government contracts for a flat fee, others typically help individual clients pursue delinquent support on a contingency fee basis. The fact that these collection agencies are in business indicates a market demand for services on collecting past due child support. If substantial fees are now levied by the public IV-D agency, the private agencies would become more attractive alternatives to custodial parents who could afford them. Once the collection of child support arrearages becomes an unsubsidized commodity, market forces would steer many custodial families to the private sector. As a result, there should be a significant decrease in IV-D caseload.

As a bureaucracy, the IV-D agency would then have a much better defined mission: to implement the standardized, relatively inexpensive enforcement activities for all custodial families, and to serve primarily lower-income families on delinquency enforcement activities. The first part of the mission is a preventive, pro-active strategy in enforcing the tax liability model of child support. The second part of the mission is the reduction of dependency on public child support.

The dividing line between "low-income" custodial families eligible for free, non-routine services and those who are not is naturally a political decision. The cut-off here should be considerably higher than the current eligibility cut-off for AFDC. An obvious reason is that many families which are not income eligible for AFDC are nonetheless not well-off by most standards. A second reason is in keeping with Greenstein's recommendation not to allow the targeted enforcement activities to become stigmatized as those "for the poorest element in society" only. In terms of budgetary concerns, the more effective the routine enforcement component, the fewer cases there are that require non-routine services, and therefore the higher the income cut-off that can be afforded.

A question of fairness

Is the targeted approach unfair to the children whose families are excluded from free non-routine services from the enforcement bureaucracy? If fairness is based on whether custodial families with different economic background should be treated in the same way, the answer is no unless we consider the pursuit of child support debts an absolute entitlement. The history of the child support system itself does not support the entitlement theory. Before the establishment of the IV-D program, all custodial parents had to hire their own lawyer to take delinquent ex-spouses to court. The system proposed here simply shifts that process to an administrative agency, and restricts the fee-for-service stipulation to families that can afford to pay.

Nonetheless, if fairness is framed in terms of the relative burden between the noncustodial and the custodial families in each case, the fee does penalize the innocent. Although the families who have to pay for services in the new system presumably are not in dire strait, the children would still be deprived of part of the resources that rightly belong to them. The same equity issue arises with private collection agencies in the current system. When a custodial family purchases the service of arrearages collection, often at a contingent fee of one-quarter or more of the final child support receipts, it is paying for the irresponsibility of the noncustodial parent. The more irresponsible the noncustodial parents, the heavier the penalty on the custodial families.

Inequity can be eliminated by shifting the penalty back where delinquency occurs, by imposing on the noncustodial parent a substantial charge on late payment.[6] Such a policy is consistent with debt payment practices in other areas of economic life, whether it is a mortgage payment or a credit card bill. Child support awards are in no way less significant than other debts and there is no reason why a parent owing child support payments should not be subject to the same consequences for delinquency.

With a late fee imposed on the noncustodial parent, custodial families seeking arrearage-collection services for a fee would not be as heavily penalized. The collection agencies, whether public or for-profit, would receive the penalty payments as part or all of their fees, thus reducing the amount the custodial parent has to pay to a small amount or even nothing. Late fee also has an important deterrence effect. It would encourage noncustodial parents to make full payments in the firs place.

This late fee should be applied to all noncustodial parents regardless of whether the custodial family is on welfare or not. Again, legislation should be passed to make universal late penalty mandatory as part of the numeric standard for determining initial award. To be realistic, the fee would have to be a percentage of the award for award amounts that are low. Since penalties that are small would not be sufficient as collection fees at for-profit agencies, the custodial families in low-award cases would have to pay out of their own pocket if they go to commercial collection services. And since award size is highly correlated with custodial family income, this system would naturally sort out those custodial families that can afford commercial services. Again this reinforces the mission of the public enforcement agency to help lower-income families in non-routine enforcement services.

Integrating Public Support

The traditional public child support system in this country is a classic example of the targeted approach. Child support assurance in its generic form advocates the universal coverage of even the public child support system. Universal coverage on both the private and public child support would deemphasize and eventually eliminate the traditional separation of enforcing private support and financing public support.

With respect to the implementation of child support assurance, such a program can be easily integrated into the model of collection and disbursement proposed in this book. As long as all private child support payments are sent to one centralized agency, that agency can determine for each payment period the amount of public supplement to which each family is entitled.

Undoubtedly some issues remain to be ironed out in a child support assurance program. The benefit may be financed solely by the federal government or jointly by a federal-state partnership; the assurance level may be uniform across the country or it may vary from state to state. The experience of the supplemental security income program, which is financed by the federal government with uniform benefit across the country but to which optional state supplementation is permitted, indicates that a centralized system of disbursement is capable of handling these variations. Therefore there is little question that the administration of the assurance benefit *can* be carried out on a universal basis. Whether it is a good policy to provide the assurance benefit as a universal or targeted benefit is a separate question.

Assurance Benefits: Universal or Targeted

One of the strengths of an assurance benefit, if available as a universal benefit for all custodial families, is that it mitigates the irregularities of private support payments. This advantage must, however, be balanced against the compelling need to contain program expenditures. The scope of coverage of the assurance benefit program is therefore primarily a function of the need for cost containment. There are basically two dimensions to this tradeoff between universal coverage and cost containment.[7]

Custodial family status

The first dimension is who should be eligible for the assured benefit. Among the current thinking on this issue, the New York Child Assistance Program represents the most targeted version of assurance programs. Since it is available only to current welfare recipients with a child support award, it restricts benefits to just a portion of the custodial parents who have very little income. This guarantees that the benefits are received by those who need them most. On the other hand, the program suffers from being associated with welfare, as well as from losing its function of guaranteeing regular payment for all children in single-parent families.

A much less categorical approach is adopted by the Wisconsin child support assurance proposal, which would use the establishment of award as the only criterion for eligibility. The Downey-Hyde proposal released in 1992 goes even further. While it uses the establishment of award as the basic criterion, it also allows for exemption by administrative law judges who can waive the requirement of actual award establishment if the custodial parent can show good cause or can demonstrate that he or she has cooperated fully in pursuing the award. Finally, universal coverage of all custodial parents regardless of whether an award is established is espoused by advocates who argue that custodial parents without an award are most in need of the assurance benefit.[8]

Not only does requiring award establishment reduce the number of families eligible, it also reduces cost indirectly by encouraging custodial parents to pursue private support awards. Without this requirement, there would be little incentive for either parent, secure in the knowledge that their children would be eligible for the assurance, to take private support obligations seriously. In order to enforce parental responsibility, therefore, the actual establishment of an award should be made a requirement, with a limited exception for extreme circumstances.

Benefit level

The second dimension in the tradeoff between universalism and cost containment is whether benefits should be reduced as the income of the custodial family increases. The need for fiscal restraint results in a custodial parent surtax in the original Wisconsin child support assurance proposal. The special tax on custodial parents would recover a portion of the assured benefits as a function of the earnings of the custodial parent, until the entire amount of the assurance benefit is phased out.

This approach unfortunately reduces the potential of income transfer to low-income families since the surtax takes effect beginning with the very first dollar of earnings. It also retains some disincentives to work, although at a much lower level than AFDC. Exempting low-income families from the surtax would alleviate this problem, but it would at the same time weaken the very concept of universality underlying the philosophy of an assurance benefit. A categorical exemption of surtax based on income criterion also runs the risk of reintroducing the stigma attached to means-tested programs. Moreover, a separate surtax on custodial parents create additional administrative chores, both for employers and for the administration of the assurance program.

An alternative would be to remove the surtax on assurance benefit but to treat the child support assurance as taxable income to the custodial family. Current law exempts child support from custodial family income for federal tax purposes. The national child support assurance program in the Downey-Hyde proposal would also designate assurance benefits as not taxable. If child support assurance benefit is made taxable, a cost containment effect similar to (but smaller than) the Wisconsin custodial parent tax could be accomplished without the complication of administering a separate tax. It also results in higher effective support for families with lower income, because of the progressive structure of the income tax system, without an explicit income test.

Among these alternatives, the Downey-Hyde proposal represents the most universal position. It also makes the strongest statement on the public's responsibility to support custodial families. With government spending as a serious political constraint, however, it is doubtful if the current form of the proposal would be enacted. Even if this proposal becomes the law, such a program runs a high risk of political backlash, as welfare in the past decade did, if private support collections turn out to be lower than expected and the cost of the program becomes unacceptable.

A slightly less universalistic approach is the above proposal to make the assurance benefit universal but taxable like other sources of income. Considering together the politics of public support, the importance of symbolizing custodial parent responsibility, as well as the simplicity of program administration, this seems to be the best compromise. This method is an improvement over the surtax on custodial income in the Wisconsin proposal since the latter leaves the vestige of a means-tested program by designating the tax-back as a custodial parent surcharge.

The universal component of the new child support system is now in place. The universal system consists of the federal collection and disbursement of child support, including both the private payment and the public assurance supplement, along with state-administered programs in universal parentage establishment and award determination. Next we will turn to the targeted component in this proposed model.

Reforming Away Welfare?

The targeted component of this proposed model consists of the non-routine functions in the child support system. These include enforcement services on past due support payments as well as employment support such as wage subsidies and social services. In order to avoid overwhelming the administrative as well as fiscal capacity of the child support system, eligibility for these support services should be based on need.

The categorical approach used to deliver these non-routine services is unlikely to undermine their political viability, however. While eligibilities are restricted, the nature of these support services encourages rather than discourages specific social values. In the case of enforcement upon delinquency, the shift towards the targeted approach allows for higher success in collecting private child support among low-income custodial families. In the case of employment support, the services encourage employment and therefore uphold parental obligations for self-sufficiency.

The model presented in this book therefore makes the routinized component of the child support system universally available to all families eligible for child support, and target the non-routine component of the system at families with lower income. Nowhere in the operation of the system would a distinction have to be made between families on welfare and those that are not. Nor would the emphasis in the new system be on the difference between enforcing private support and financing public support. This would immunize the new system from the stigma or the strong disincentive to work associated with the traditional welfare system.

The welfare system would still exist alongside this new model, however, although that system would hopefully be considerably smaller in the long-run. Results of the simulation reported in chapter 5 indicate that we should not be overly optimistic in the capacity of the universal component of the new child support system in reducing the size of the AFDC program. The extent of reduction is in fact contingent on the public's willingness to provide targeted support services to assist low-income custodial families in their quest for self-sufficiency.

David Ellwood has recommended the replacement of the current welfare system with a new system where financial assistance is of a short duration, up to two or three years.[9] When eligibility for assistance runs out, welfare recipients would be provided with jobs rather than further welfare benefits:

> I surmise that only a tiny fraction would actually need these jobs if the other reforms were in place. Remember that single mothers with child support would not have to work more than half time to avoid poverty. Remember, too, that they would have had two or three years to adjust to their new situation, acquiring training and transitional support, and move to a part-time job in the private sector. But for those who could not make it with child support, medical care, and transitional assistance, I think it is reasonable to say, "We have a job for you if you want it, but you cannot collect cash aid indefinitely."[10]

This approach pushes the argument for employment support one step further. The public would provide support services to help custodial parents find work during the transitional period when benefits are awarded. Failing that, actual employments would be given in place of welfare assistance. President Clinton has made this approach part of his plan to reform the welfare system during his election campaign in 1992.

No singular strategy will ever reform the welfare system successfully. If concerted strategies are developed to enhance the capacity of government policy to uphold parental as well as public obligations to children in single-parent household, however, we will gradually restrain dependency on the current welfare system, and in due time, actually reduce it.

These strategies must include the universal enforcement and financing of child support responsibilities. An effective administrative network involving the cooperation between federal and state governments is an essential part of these universal child support functions. In addition, resources targeted at the more needy custodial families must be available to help them discharge their financial and care-taking responsibility to the children. Although not covered in this book, preventive strategies that reduce the incidence of nonmarital teenage childbearing would be instrumental as well.

None of these will be easy. If past history is any indication, it will take a few years for these strategies to be in place, and quite a few more years before any results will be visible. Fortunately the consensus about mutual reciprocity is here. Maybe the day will approach when almost every child knows who the parents are and be supported by both of them even if he or she may not be living with both of them; maybe the day will approach when almost no children will live in a family that depends on AFDC for a long time.

Notes for Chapter 7

1. William Julius Wilson, *The Truly Disadvantaged: The Inner City, the Underclass, and Public Policy* (Chicago, IL: University of Chicago Press, 1987); Theda Skocpol, "Targeting within Universalism: Politically viable Policies to Combat Poverty in the United States," in Chistopher Jencks and Paul Peterson, eds., *The Urban Underclass* (Washington, DC: Brookings Institution, 1991); Irwin Garfinkel, ed., *Income-Tested Transfer Programs: The Case For and Against* (New York, NY: Academic Press, 1982).

2. Robert Greenstein, "Universal and Targeted Approaches to Relieving Poverty: An Alternative View," in Christopher Jencks and Paul Peterson, eds., *The Urban Underclass*.

3. *Ibid.*, p. 450.

4. Federal law allows the state to charge a non-welfare custodial family a fee up to $25, but many states waive the fee.

5. The incentive payments are the same for AFDC and non-AFDC cases subject to the limit that the incentive payments based on non-AFDC collections may not exceed 115 percent of those based on the state's AFDC collections.

6. Richard C. Hoffman, "Crack Down on Deadbeat Dads," *New York Times*, December 5, 1992, p.15.

7. See also Daniel R. Meyer, Irwin Garfinkel, Donald T. Oellerich, and Philip K. Robin, "Who Should be Eligible for an Assured Child Support Benefit?" in Irwin Garfinkel, Sara S. McLanahan, and Philip K. Robins, eds., *Child Support Assurance:Design Issues, Expected Impacts, and Political Barriers as Seen from Wisconsin* (Washington, DC: Urban Institute Press, 1992); and David T. Ellwood, *Poor Support: Poverty in the American Family* (New York: Basic Books, 1988), pp. 169-174 for discussions of similar issues.

8. Paula Roberts, "Child Support and Beyond: Mapping a Future for America's Low-income Children," *Clearinghouse Review* (November 1988), p. 597.

9. David T. Ellwood, *Poor Support: Poverty in the American Family*, p. 179.

10. *Ibid.*, p. 180.

Appendix

Simulation of Public Child Support Reform

This Appendix describes the methodology adopted to simulate the effects of the Wisconsin Child Support Assurance System (CSAS).[1] For the purpose of this simulation, CSAS consists of these elements:

(1) A percentage-of-income standard to determine support obligation.
(2) Immediate and universal wage withholding to collect child support payments.
(3) New public support programs: child support assurance (CSA) and work expense offset (WEO).

The simulation includes four component parts: predicting noncustodial parents' income, estimating probability of obtaining an award for each custodial family in the data sample, estimating the proportion of award that will be collected from noncustodial parents, and predicting custodial parents' decision on labor supply and program participation given the availability of the new programs.

Information on noncustodial parents' income is necessary so that the percentage of income standard can be used to determine the amount of private child support in each case. However, since data sets on custodial parents typically do not contain information on income, it is estimated on the basis of individual custodial family characteristics. The procedures for this step are described by Garfinkel and Oellerich.[2]

With the income estimate for each noncustodial parent, the size of private child support awards under the new percentage income standard can be computed. Under the standard, child support obligation is 17 percent of gross income for one child. For two to five or more children, they are 25, 29, 31, and 34 percents respectively. Since the number of children owed child support is a variable in the custodial parent data sets, total support obligation can easily be computed.

Because the availability of child support assurance is likely to encourage custodial parents' efforts in seeking awards and because immediate withholding enhances the efficiency of collection, CSAS is expected to result in both more awards and higher collections. If we could assume that all custodial parents succeed in obtaining award and that all noncustodial parents make full payments, then we would simply assign 100 percent of the estimated child support obligation to each family in the data set. Yet no matter how well the new system performs, no one envisions the securing of awards for all eligible families nor the collection of all payments awarded.

The simulation must therefore (1) account for the imperfect improvement in award and (2) account for imperfect improvement in collections, before proceeding to (3) predict the change in work effort by custodial parents in response to the new policy. This Appendix describes the method used in each of these three steps.

Estimating Child Support Award

Some custodial families in the data set do not currently have an award. Similarly a (smaller) portion of them are not expected to have an award even under CSAS. The crudest way to account for this in the simulation would be to ignore a random portion of the no-award cases in the data set; or, in order to retain all cases, to discount the weight of all no-award cases by the same proportion. Yet a better way is to look at whether there are demographic characteristics that distinguish custodial families with and without awards.

At the national level, marital status of the custodial mother makes a big difference--76 percent of those divorced or remarried, 61 percent of those separated, and only 18 percent of never-married mothers--have awards in 1983. There are also important racial differences. Sixty-seven percent of whites but 34 percent of blacks have awards. Thus if the known current status of award can be related to the characteristics of custodial families in our sample, we will be able to account for different probabilities of obtaining awards by demographic characteristics.

Predicting award probability

To accomplish this the subsample of cases in the data set that have a current award are selected. A probit equation is estimated according to

(Eqn 1) $E(A) = \underline{b} * \underline{X}$

> where A = 1 if current award exists,
>   0 otherwise;
> $\underline{X}$ = vector of demographic attributes,
> $\underline{b}$ = vector of coefficients.

and the probability of award is

$$P(A) = \frac{EXP[E(A)]}{1 + EXP[E(A)]}$$

This probability is now computed for each custodial family on the basis of the custodial family vector $\underline{X}$. Thus some fraction, reflected by P(A), of each case in our sample represents some families in the population of custodial families with a child support award; the rest of that case, 1 - P(A), represents families with no award at all. Since a family without a child support award does not enter the reform system, the sample weight of each family is discounted by the estimated probability of not having an award. The total sum of the new weights in the data represents expected incidence of child support awards by demographic groups in the current system.

Improving award probability

The child support assurance system is expected to result in the inclusion of more eligible families into the child support system. This means that the simulation should incorporate a higher probability of award than is currently the case. In the absence of a reliable estimate on the extent of the increase in award incidence, we carry out several simulations assuming "low," "medium," and "high" improvements in the system are carried out.

Each of these three regimes represents a percentage increase in award probability relative to the current baseline. For custodial parents who are never married or are separated, the three regimes are represented by improvement of 50 percent, 75 percent, and 100 percent respectively over the current award rate. For divorced and remarried custodial parents who tend to have a higher award rate to begin with, lower improvement rates of 25, 27.5, and 30 percents are used.

Estimating Child Support Collection Rate

Even after a family has secured an award for child support, its collection is not a certainty. Only half of those mothers with awards in 1983 managed to collect the full amount due them. One way of accounting for this inefficiency is to discount the aggregate child support collected by a fixed percentage across the board. Again, it is possible to get a better estimate by using a statistical model.

Estimating collection rate

An ordinary least square (OLS) procedure is used on the entire sample of custodial families. Current child support payment rate is estimated as:

(Eqn. 4.3) $E(C) = \underline{a} * \underline{Y}$

> where C = the percentage of support paid,
> $\underline{Y}$ = vector of demographic attributes,
> $\underline{a}$ = vector of coefficients.

Improving collection rate

This collection fraction is raised in postulated "low," "medium," and "high" improvement regimes by upward adjustment of the intercept and slope of the regression equation. The predicted private child support amount can now be multiplied by this collection fraction at the micro-level.

The improvement regimes are represented by raising the intercept of the estimated OLS equation. For the Wisconsin data set, the intercept is 0.39. The low improvement regime raises the intercept to 0.50. Medium improvement corresponds to an intercept of 0.60; and for high improvement, 0.70. In addition, a maximum collection of 95 percent is assumed for all cases.

Model of Labor Supply Response to Reform

The Child Support Assurance System makes available a set of economic incentives very different from the existing welfare system. Relative to the latter, CSAS has a lower tax rate. It also subsidizes work through the work expense offset. Some of the custodial parents currently on welfare are therefore expected to opt for more work and to leave welfare. At the same time, many of those not on welfare will experience an increase in unearned income through either increased private child support payment or the assured benefit which may reduce their work effort. This section describes the methodology involved in the empirical assessment of the change in labor supply in each group.

The first section below presents the theoretical model in predicting a custodial parent's work effort. The second section describes how incomplete variables are treated. Then the procedures for implementing the model are set forth in the last three sections, including the selection of empirical estimates for the model, adjusting the model to account for unobserved differences in preference, and the final computation on program and labor supply decisions.

Program structure

When CSAS is implemented, custodial families have three program options: (1) To receive benefits from the existing AFDC program, (2) To receive benefits from the CSAS reform, and (3) To receive neither. Program choice is voluntary except for those whose unearned income are too high to be eligible for either of the first two options no matter how work behavior is changed. In order to predict the labor supply and program participation decisions, it is necessary to first characterize the program options available to a family.

For simplicity, it is assumed in the following characterization that the custodial family has no unearned income other than child support and welfare, and that it faces no income and payroll taxes. These restrictions do not affect the model and are relaxed in actual research implementation.

The AFDC option

If the family opts for the AFDC program, its benefits are determined according to the following formula:

$$AFDC = \begin{cases} TA-t_AWH-TC+Dis & \text{if } WH < (TA-TC+Dis)/t_A \\ 0 & \text{if } WH \geq (TA-TC+Dis)/t_A \end{cases}$$

where AFDC = the AFDC benefit,
       TA = the AFDC guarantee,
       t_A = the AFDC tax rate,[3]
       W = custodial parent's wage rate,
       H = hours of work,
       TC = custodial parent's private child support receipt,
       Dis = the $50 monthly set-aside of private child support, if applicable
$(G_A-CS_H+Dis)/t_A$ = the breakeven level of AFDC.

Under current federal legislation, private child support payment TC is taxed at the rate of 100% after the first $50 set-aside. If the AFDC option is chosen, any TC or assured benefits received are treated like other unearned income and the reform system is irrelevant.

The CSAS option

The Wisconsin CSAS has the following features. For incomes up to one-half the maximum income for eligibility (Y_C), the custodial parent is eligible for a work expense offset of S per hour. The income of the custodial parent (unsubsidized earnings plus nonwage income) is taxed at the same rate as the uniform percentage standard applied to the noncustodial parent's income. For incomes above half the income cap, the work expense offset is taxed away at such a rate that when total income reaches the cap, the family is no longer eligible for a subsidy. If the family opts for the CSAS instead of the AFDC program, it will receive benefits according to the following formula:

$$CS_T = \begin{cases} G_C + (S\text{-}t_CW)H - TC & \text{if } Y < .5\,Y_C \\ G^*_C + (S\text{-}t_CW\text{-}t_WW)H - TC & \text{if } .5Y_C < Y < Y_C \\ 0 & \text{if } Y > Y_C \end{cases}$$

where CS_T = the total public child support benefit,

   TC = custodial parent private support,

   TB = the assured benefit,

   S = the hourly wage subsidy,

   t_C = the custodial parent tax rate,

   Y = total family income,

   Y_C = the income cap for public child support eligibility,

   t_W = the tax rate that must be applied to the unsubsidized wage to phase out the total CS_T benefit at Y_C,

   G^*_C = virtual nonwage income associated with the work expense offset segment of the budget line.[4]

Like the AFDC program, CSAS only pays benefits in excess of the amount of child support received through wage withholding. In other words, like AFDC, it taxes TC at the rate of 100%. But it taxes other sources of income only at the rate of t_C. As long as t_C is lower than the AFDC tax rate t_A, CSAS provides higher incentive to work. The above equation indicates that CSAS can be characterized by a budget line with a convex kink at $1/2Y_C$ and a nonconvex kink at Y_C.

The leisure-income preference model

In order to simulate labor supply response to CSAS, it is necessary to specify a labor supply decision model. The characterization of the AFDC and CSAS programs just described provides a useful framework for a labor supply decision model based on the assumption of utility maximization. Referring again to Figure 6.1, if work hours are chosen to be greater than H_3, the family's choice is not to receive either CSAS or AFDC benefits. If labor supply is between H_K and H_3, the family chooses to receive CSAS benefits. When work hours are between H_1 and H_2, the family would still be eligible for AFDC benefits. However, the family would choose CSAS in this case because of the high tax rate under AFDC. Finally, if labor supply is less than H_1, the family chooses to participate in the AFDC program.

The analysis of Figure 5.1 suggests that variables determining preferences (shapes of indifference curves) and parameters of the AFDC and CSAS programs (G_A, t_A, G_C, t_C, and the size of the wage subsidy) will determine labor supply and, hence, program participation. Extending the analysis of Burtless and Hausman[5] to a four segment budget line, we can write the indirect utility function as $V_i(w_i, n_i)$, where V is utility, w_i is the net wage rate along budget segment i, and n_i is nonwage (or virtual) income along budget segment i. Under the assumption of utility maximization, the program participation and labor supply decisions can be written as follows:

$$V^* = \quad \text{Max}(V_1, V_2, V_3, V_4)$$

$$H = \begin{cases} f(W(1\text{-}t_A), TA) & \text{if} \quad V^* = V_1 \\ f(S+W(1\text{-}t_C), TB) & \text{if} \quad V^* = V_2 \\ f(S+W(1\text{-}t_C\text{-}t_W), G^*_C) & \text{if} \quad V^* = V_3 \\ f(W, TC) & \text{if} \quad V^* = V_4 \end{cases}$$

Upon specifying a utility model as a function of labor and income, the indirect utility function and the labor supply function can be derived. Program participation and labor supply decision of each family can then be predicted.

Tax rates

Various tax rates are involved in simulating the budget options. The custodial parent surtax is fixed as a function of the number of children for all families. Another tax, the work expense offset tax-back rate, is set to mathematically eliminate benefits at a set level of income; it can be analytically derived for each family's specific economic situation. Other tax rates do not have such unambiguous solutions. The following paragraphs outline the treatment of each relevant tax rate in the labor supply simulation.

The first is the tax rate faced by recipients of the welfare program. Statutory tax rate is 100 percent for those who have been on welfare for four or more months. The rate is lower for new participants because of the thirty-and-a-third disregard rule. In practice, however, allowable work expense and child care deductions result in an effective tax rate lower than the statutory rate in each case. To take into account this effective rate, we use the estimate derived by Fraker et al[6] of 68 percent for Wisconsin recipients after the fourth month. It is also assumed that all custodial parents face the post-four-month welfare option. This eliminates the problem of having to simulate a budget set changing over time. Our simulation therefore implies a long-term, steady-state policy environment.

All custodial parents also face income and payroll taxes. For the latter we use the statutory rate of 7.15 percent throughout the earnings scale, ignoring the absence of payroll tax at high earnings level. This should be harmless in view of the generally low earnings capacity of the target population. Also, for individuals at such high earnings level, eligibility for either of the two public programs is nullified.

Income tax is more problematic. The simplest possible solution is chosen. First, state income tax is ignored because of its relatively small impact. Federal income tax rate is also assumed away for those on welfare, and arbitrarily set at a uniform rate of 10 percent upon termination of AFDC for work.[7] For the non-AFDC group, federal tax rate is calculated for each family with the following assumptions. All families are assumed to use the standard rather than itemized deductions; only members in the nuclear families are claimed as dependent exemptions; and married couples file jointly. This way the marginal tax rate as well as current tax liability of the family are calculated as a function solely of marital status and family size.

For the sake of simplicity, once the initial marginal tax rate is obtained, it is used throughout the simulation and the progressivity of the tax structure is ignored. The effect of this simplification is that custodial parents reducing their work effort (the non-AFDC group) faces a higher than actual tax rate, while the tax rate faced by the welfare recipients opting for the alternative program is lower than in reality. In view of the fact that even among families leaving AFDC, the average increase in earnings is less than $3,000, this favorable tax treatment should not affect the accuracy of the simulation.

Selecting the empirical utility function

Implementing the labor supply and program participation model requires empirically based estimates of a utility function. Rather than deriving such estimates directly, we draw on results from the existing labor supply literature. For purposes of this study, the results obtained by Johnson and Pencavel[8] in their analysis of the labor supply response to the Seattle and Denver Income Maintenance Experiments are used. There are two reasons for this choice. The first is the comparability of the study sample. Separate results are reported in that study for female heads of family, a group very similar to our custodial parents in Wisconsin. The second is a good match between variables, since all the pertinent variables in the Johnson-Pencavel model are contained in the Wisconsin data files of custodial families with which this simulation model was first implemented.

The direct utility function estimated in their study is of the Stone-Geary form and can be written as follows:

$$U(C,H) = .872\ln(C/m+2776) + .128\ln(2151-H/r),$$

where C = annual consumption of market goods,
H = annual hours of work,
m = 1 - .401ln(1+K), K being the number of children in the family under 18,
r = 1 - .071P, P being 1 if there are pre-school children, 0 otherwise.

Maximization of this equation subject to the budget line

$$C = n + WH$$

where n = annual unearned income,
w = net hourly wage rate,

yields the following optimal labor supply function:

$H^* = 1876r - (.128n - 355m)/w.$

Substituting this labor supply function into the direct utility function $U(C,H)$ yields the indirect utility function:

$$V(w,n) = .872 * \ln((.872n + 1876rw + 355m)/m + 2776)$$
$$+ .128 * \ln(275 + (.128n - 355m)/rw).$$

The indirect utility function is used as an index to compare the level of satisfaction from participating in each program option. The option yielding the highest satisfaction is chosen, and the associated hours of work and level of income are used to generate the predicted effects of the CSAS. The procedure for generating the predictions first involves a modification of the above empirical model, to be explained below.

Respecification of the utility model

A custodial parent's current labor supply as observed in the data file will not, in general, be the same as the utility-maximizing labor supply computed from the equation of H*. One way of explaining this is to treat it as a measurement error in the observed hour. Another way is to attribute it to factors left out of the utility function. In any event a simulation based on a utility model at variance with current behavior would give uninterpretable results. To solve this problem, an error term is appended to that equation to make the observed hours of work consistent with the optimal hours of work. This error term is best thought of as describing the unobservable preference for (or aversion to) work of each family.

For current workers in the sample the error term is the simple difference between the observed hour H_o and the theoretical optimal hour H^*: $e = H_o - H^*$. Appending the error term results in a taste-adjusted optimal labor supply of $H' = H^* + e = H_o$.

However, this procedure causes problems for non-workers because they are not generally on the margin of going to work. For them the optimal labor supply equation H^* is inapplicable. Their implied optimal hour from the model must be arrived at through an iterative process using current unearned income and tax rates. This implied optimal hour H^* may take on positive or negative value. But the true optimal hours of work for these persons must be non-positive although only a zero H_o is observed. This is a version of a truncation problem that occurs when the desired value cannot be observed beyond a point.

To deal with this problem, a stochastic error term is introduced. The error term e is assumed to be distributed normally with a mean of zero and a standard deviation of 990 hours per year.[9] Then a value for e is randomly selected from a truncated normal distribution to ensure that the optimal hours of work are less than or equal to zero. That is, choose e from the distribution e $N(0,990)$ such that the optimal hour is defined as $H' = H^* + e \leq 0$, or $e \leq -H^*$. The negative optimal hour H' may be thought of as a measure of the inertia to be overcome to start working.

With the error term specified for both workers and non-workers, the labor supply function can be rewritten as

$$H' = 1876r - (.128n - 355m)/w + e,$$

and the total optimal consumption for the custodial family becomes

$$c' = \begin{cases} n + wH' & \text{if } H' > 0 \\ n & \text{if } H' \leq 0. \end{cases}$$

With these solutions, a displaced utility level $U(C',H') = U(n+w(H^*+e), H^*+e)$ is obtained, representing the adjusted optimal level of utility attained by each individual after these differences are taken into account.

Computation of utility on each budget option

Now all families are at their optimal income-leisure choice before the reform. Simulation may proceed for calculating the optimal utility that each family can attain from each budget option made available by the reform.

Referring back to Figure 5.1, there are four budget segments to choose from along the kinked budget set AGKED. The optimal hour of work on each of these segments is obtained by substituting into the optimal hours of work equation the values of (1) the family's economic position -- gross wage rate, private unearned income; (2) appropriate policy parameters -- AFDC guarantee, Child Support Assurance, the various tax rates; and (3) the error term. The associated utility level can then be solved numerically for each budget segment. The highest utility level defines the family's postprogram labor supply and program participation status.

Notes for Appendix

1. See Pat Wong, *The Economic Effects of the Wisconsin Child Support Assurance System: A Simulation Study with a Labor Supply Model* (Madison, WI: University of Wisconsin Unpublished Dissertation, 1988), Chapter 4.

2. Irwin Garfinkel and Donald T. Oellerich, "Noncustodial Father's Ability to Pay Child Support" in Irwin Garfinkel, Sara S. McLanahan, and Philip K. Robins, eds., *Child Support Assurance: Design Issues, Expected Impacts, and Political Barriers as Seen from Wisconsin* (Washington, DC: Urban Institute Press, 1992).

3. The statutory tax rate of the AFDC program is 100% after four months of work. Since work expenses and child care are deducted from earnings, however, the effective tax rate t_A is less than 100%.

4. As illustrated in to Figure 6.1, virtual income is where the extension of EK meets the income axis on the left side of the graph, that is, when projected to zero hours of work. This value is not visible to the family but is analytically required to specify the budget option for utility maximization computations. See Gary Burtless and Jerry A. Hausman, "The Effect of Taxation on Labor Supply: Evaluating the Gary Negative Income Tax Experiment," *Journal of Political Economy* 86 (1978): 1103-1130.

5. Ibid.

6. Thomas Fraker, Robert Moffitt, and Douglas Wolf, "Effective Tax Rates in the AFDC Program," *Journal of Human Resources* 20 (1985):251-263.

7. If marginal tax rates were computed individually for each AFDC family, the majority would have a pre-reform tax rate of zero. Using a zero income tax rate for welfare families in simulating the alternatives would make the CSAS reform unjustifiably attractive relative to welfare. Therefore the tax rate is arbitrarily set at 10%. It turns out that moving this rate up or down 5% does not appreciably alter the results.

8. Terry R. Johnson and John H. Pencavel, "Dynamic Hours of Work Functions for Husbands, Wives, and Single Females," *Econometrica* 52 (1984): 363-389.

9. This standard deviation is taken from Michael C. Keeley, Philip K. Robins, Robert G. Spiegelman and Richard W. West, "The Estimation of Labor Supply Models Using Experimental Data," *American Economic Review* 68 (1978): 873-887, who review the experimental literature on labor supply and conclude that 990 hours per year is a rough average across studies. Johnson and Pencavel (Ibid.) do not present standard deviation for their estimation.

Index